MW01144162

OLD AND YOUNG AHEAD

OLD AND YOUNG AHEAD

by Abram Kean

Flanker Press Ltd.
St. John's, Newfoundland
2000

Published in Canada by Flanker Press Ltd.
P O Box 2522, Station C, St. John's
Newfoundland, Canada A1C 6K1

Tel/Fax (709) 739-4477
email: info@flankerpress.com
Website: www.flankerpress.com

Cover design and book layout by Jerry Cranford

The publisher wishes to thank Carolyn (Gosse) Morgan and
Madeline (Kean) Gosse for their assistance in procuring
additional photographs.

Canadian Cataloguing in Publication Data

Kean, Abram, 1855-1945.

Old and young ahead

Reprint, with some additions, of the ed. published:
        London : Heath, Cranton, 1935.
Includes index.
ISBN 1-894463-06-4

1. Kean, Abram, 1855-1945. 2. Sealers (Persons) --
Newfoundland -- Biography. 3. Sealing -- Newfoundland --
History. 4. Politicians -- Newfoundland -- Biography. I. Title

FC2173.1.K42A3 1999   971.8'02'092   C99-950196-8
F1123.K42 1999

FOREWORD

When Captain Abram Kean, doyen of our ice hunters and northern seamen, invited me to write a foreword to his book, I felt profoundly honoured, for we have been friends for forty years, and I know what he has consistently stood for among our northern seafaring people. True seamanship—courage—unselfishness, and genuine love for his fellow men. To the American public and the world "Captain Bob" has introduced those yeomen of our fisheries, the Bartlett family. I am hoping this book will introduce another than whom none are better loved and trusted in the North. Somehow it may, I hope, lead to a better appreciation of the character developed in what is regarded by some as a "humble calling." There are many such yeomen in the North. It was to men of such calling Christ Himself entrusted the ineffable message He came to earth to reveal. A gale of wind in the winter in the North Atlantic when your sheets are frozen solid, your canvas blown to ribbons, and you have no way of knowing where you are in a heavily laden small schooner with all your own and perhaps your best loved one aboard off an ill-charted coast makes one feel humble in the presence of the unseen—and yet all that is manly and noble is challenged. "They that go down to the sea in ships" don't often write books; when they do I advise all my friends, especially professional story-writers, to read them. I heartily recommend Captain Kean's book to every one of them.

WILFRED GRENFELL

ABRAM KEAN

INTRODUCTION

Captain Abram Kean

Abram Kean was born 8 July 1855 at Flowers Island, Bonavista Bay, to Joseph and Jane Kean - the youngest of nine children in a family of sealers and cod fishers. Unlike the other members his family who were illiterate, Abram received about three years of regular classroom education. His mother died when he was thirteen and his father hired a housekeeper, Caroline Yetman. At the age of seventeen, Abram married Ms. Yetman who was seven years older. They had eight children - six sons and two daughters.

At the age of thirteen, Abram became a cod fisherman with his brothers and at the age of 23, commanded a fishing schooner. In 1879, he moved his family off Flowers Island to nearby Norton's Cove (which he renamed Brookfield) on the mainland. As a northeast coast fisherman, it was only natural for Abram to go sealing every spring, and he worked his way up through the ranks from common hand to master watch, second hand (as the first mates were called) and, finally, to captain of the family schooner *Peerless*. However, with the introduction of the first steamers in 1863, the number of sailing vessels prosecuting the seal fishery declined rapidly. Thus, in 1884, Abram applied for and received the position of bridge master on the steamer *Ranger*, under the command of Captain Joe Barbour.

In 1885, Kean was elected to the legislature as a Reform Party member for Bonavista, but he did not run in the next election in 1889. He moved his family to St. John's in 1887 and soon qualified for his Master's Certificate. In 1889, he commanded the *SS Wolf* at the seal fishery, and in a record-setting eleven days, he brought in 26,912 seal pelts. With this promising start, he began a career as sealing captain that lasted until his retirement in 1936.

In addition to being a professional sealing captain, Kean excelled in other areas as well. He served a second term as a legislator, representing Bay de Verde as a conservative in the Winter government of 1897-1900. During this administration, he was chosen by Prime Minister Winter as the first minister of the newly-created Department of Marine and Fisheries. In 1927, he was appointed to the Legislative Council, where he served until the Council's dissolution in 1934. Furthermore, for about nineteen years, he was involved with Bowring Brothers' coastal boat service, usually in charge, and served as captain. And he spent approximately in the cod fishery. Finally, he wrote his autobiography, and his name must be added to that very select number of Newfoundlanders to do so. However, it was as a sealing captain that he was most widely known and respected.

Kean was captain of a sealing steamer every year from his command of the *Wolf* in 1889 until his retirement after the 1936 sealing season, with one exception - 1896. He commanded nine steamers: *Wolf, Hope, Aurora, Terra Nova, Florizel, Stephano, Nascopie, Thetis* and *Beothic II*. He set the record for the number of seal pelts brought in from one voyage when he brought in 49,069 pelts in 1910. This record remained unbroken until 1933, when Captain Albert Blackwood brought in 55,636 pelts in the vastly superior *SS Imogene*. However, Kean set the overall record for seal pelts landed over a lifetime - 1,052,737 - breaking the million mark in 1934. He was awarded the O.B.E. in the summer of that year. He spent his most productive years commanding steamers belonging to Bowring Brothers, including the huge *Stephano* and *Florizel*. And he retired from sealing as an employee of that firm at the age of 81.

Kean did not enjoy a trouble-free life. He was in business for about fourteen years but does not appear to have been too successful. As a young boy he accidently shot and killed his three-year-old nephew. Also, as mentioned, his mother died when he was only thirteen, and there were other tragic deaths in his family. In fact, he took in and supported the families of two of his brothers so that he "had eleven others besides my own family to provide for." Certainly, he was a generous soul.

Kean's reputation has suffered from a couple of sealing tragedies in which he was involved. The first involved 48 casualties from the crew of the *SS Greenland* in 1898. It was rumoured that Kean's crew had stolen pelts belonging to the Greenland's crew, who were thereby forced to continue sealing and were caught out in a storm. The second tragedy concerned the *SS Newfoundland's* crew in 1914. He had taken them on board his own vessel, the *Stephano*, and steamed to a place where he thought they could find seals and then dropped them off. A snow storm descended and when it was all over, 78 men were dead and many maimed. Kean was accused of putting the men overboard in a storm and also of misjudging the location, thus confusing the men when they tried to walk back to their own steamer. Although in fairness to Kean, he was not a highly educated man, and it is likely that the direction in which he steamed on that fateful occasion could have been off his intended course. In fact, the main cause of the tragedy was the removal of the wireless equipment from the *Newfoundland* as a cost-cutting measure; Kean and his son, Westbury, captain of the *Newfoundland*, unable to communicate with each other, each thought the missing men were on board the other steamer. Nonetheless, it is this tragedy that has affected Kean's reputation the most. But despite the disfavour with which he is often viewed today, it is important to recognize that many sealers wanted to serve under Kean's command because they respected him as a successful captain.

This book was published under the title *Old and Young Ahead* - the cry often heard when the sealing ship came onto a patch of seals. It is an interesting and informative book but somewhat idiosyncratic and opinionated - after all Kean was almost eighty years old when he wrote it. Thus, his memory fails him on occasion, and in addition, he does not give his sealing career the prominence it deserves. The latter is understandable because, to him, it was just a job - although a well paid one. Consequently, he occasionally dwells on issues that are less interesting to the present-day reader. Nevertheless, this is the first-hand account of sealing of Newfoundland's greatest sealing captain and is intrinsically valuable because of that.

A note to readers: While "Abram" is the accepted spelling of his name, one often sees it spelt elsewhere as "Abraham." For example, a lecture he delivered on the seal fishery to the Newfoundland Historical Society in 1921 was printed as being delivered by Abraham Kean; his commission to serve in the Royal Naval Reserve in 1917 also used the latter spelling. In addition, the text that follows is exactly as Kean published it, but the current editor has added a number of explanatory notes and [sic] references. Kean, himself, provided only one explanatory note - the first end note at the end of Chapter VI.

S. R.

CONTENTS

Sailing vessel of the old type

S.S. Portia

S.S. TERRA-NOVA

S.S. AURORA

CHAPTER I

Early life on Flowers Island—The family business—Illness and death—The break-up of a partnership—My first trip to the seal fishery—Marriage at seventeen—Death of my father

On the 8th day of July, 1855, I first saw the light of day, and exactly seventy-nine years later to the day I decided to write the history of my own life. In this year of grace, 1934, however, I brought into my country my millionth seal.[1] This was done in the ships that I have commanded during forty-five consecutive years, and marks the culmination of a life-work. My fellow countrymen, almost to a man, have offered their congratulations. It seems fitting to commence writing an account of my own life on my seventy-ninth birthday.

I was born at Flowers Island, which is composed of two islands about five miles from the mainland, on the north side of Bonavista Bay. No doubt it was called Flowers Island on account of the profusion of flowers that grow on these two islands in the summer season. The larger of these two islands was called Sturge's Island as it was inhabited by men of that name, with the exception of one man whose name was Mahre, who married a Sturge and settled down there. The smaller island was called Kean's Island and inhabited by three brothers of that name and their families. I was the youngest son of Joseph and Jane Kean. My father, who was by no means a rich man, was always independent and his children never knew want. The family consisted of nine children, six sons and three daughters.

Unfortunately, there was no school on these islands, and I was the only one born on either of them who could read or write until long after I became a man. I shall tell you later of how I succeeded in having a school set up on our island.

In order to give a complete picture of my life it is necessary to say something of my stock. My father, when quite a young man, entered into partnership with my Uncle William, a man remarkable for his perseverance, initiative and energy, who probably had more to do with moulding and shaping my destiny than my father. In the agreement they entered into as young men, it was agreed that my uncle would pursue the seal fishery in vessels and that my father should look after sealing on shore.[2] My father was a martyr to rheumatism, and this accounted for his decision to stay on land.

My uncle very soon distinguished himself at the seal fishery. He became the very successful master of a sailing vessel, and was one of the first to command a steamer in 1863. My father and mother seemed to have decided that they would make me an exception to the rule among their children. I, being the youngest, was to be sent to school.

I was less than eight years old, and when my father was about to leave me, I broke down with home-sickness and cried bitterly to go back again to Flowers Island, which I thought then was the most beautiful spot on earth. The man who was to teach me was about sixty-three years old. When he appeared on the scene he told my father he ought to take a piece of rope and give me a whipping. As can be imagined, this beginning to my schooldays was anything but pleasant. There was, however, one redeeming feature—my uncle had something of the milk of human kindness in his breast and took kindly to me. Very soon he assumed the rôle of uncle and father, and this cured me of my nostalgia. I soon learned that there was rivalry in school, and in a very short time I was doing my best to lead. I succeeded in doing so.

My stay with my uncle lasted less than two years, during which time we learned to love each other like David and

Jonathan. When school was over in the afternoon I made a bee-line for my uncle. I always longed to hear something of his past history and of his exploits at the seal fishery in particular. In telling me these stories he did not treat me as a boy but as if I were in every way his equal. Many of the things he told me about seals and their habits have remained in my memory, and I have since proved their accuracy.

But Nemesis was on my track. Before I had been two years with my uncle and before I was ten years old I went back to Flowers Island to spend my holidays there. In handling a gun there, I met with tragedy. I shot my hand and at the same time killed my brother's son, a little boy three years and nine months old. I was so fond of him that this accident absolutely unnerved me. So much so that I did not go back again to my uncle's, but later that year went to school at Greenspond with my married sister. I had been at school with my first teacher one and a half years, and when I went to school at Greenspond the boys asked me how far I was in arithmetic. I did not even know the meaning of the word! Altogether I was at school four years, but the delay caused by the tragic accident gave me only three years' tuition, except for what I acquired as an adult.

I arrived back from school on the 1st day of May, 1867, which made altogether four years to a day from the time I left my home to go with my uncle. I was then nearing twelve years of age. My home-coming was marred considerably by learning that my mother was nearing her end.

My father, who was very much upset over my mother's illness, decided that I should read a portion of Scripture or some other good book to her once every day. I gladly agreed to do so for I loved my parents dearly, as I had good reason to believe that they were the best parents in the world. Every day at about eleven o'clock I could be found at my mother's beside reading to her, with my father an ardent listener. This lasted about three months, and then that dread disease claimed her as its own. Thus at the age of fifty-four my mother gave us a parting farewell. The union

3

between my father and mother was a very loving one, and she was a most devoted mother to her children. Every mother on the two islands wept bitterly when she died, each declaring she was the best friend she ever had.

Thus at the age of thirteen a new chapter opened for me. My mother was gone, my father and my brothers and sisters had no education and did not know its value. I had no trouble in making my father and the family believe that there was no need for me to go back to school. Many of my readers well can imagine how bitterly I regretted this decision in after life. The most I could hope for was that the day would come when I might have charge of a fishing schooner like my elder brothers or, best of all, become master of a sailing vessel at the seal fishery like my uncle. This, then, was the height of my ambition.

I have often thought what a blessing it is that we cannot see into the future. As it is, the troubles that come to us seem to fit the back for the burden. Up to the time when I had met with the accident of killing my brother's son, death had not invaded our home for years and we were a happy family, but the father of the boy who was killed, our eldest brother and skipper, was brought home from the Labrador one year after his son's death and died before he reached home, leaving a wife and two small children, who were afterwards to become my care.

The following year my mother died. 1870 was also memorable. My third eldest brother, Joseph, developed a disease in the lower part of the body and for two years suffered extreme pain. For fifteen years he was unable to walk, and during all that time he was incapable of even sitting in a chair. His wife and son died; he had one daughter. I took him into my home and my wife superintended the nursing of the daughter, who was young and needed her care and attention. After two years of pain, however, he obtained relief from suffering but was unable to walk. In many respects he was the most interesting person I have ever known. His name went far, and during his illness thousands flocked to see him—not to bring him consolation but to take comfort away with them. Not only was he patient in his suffering, but being of a pleasant disposition, he saw the bright side of everything, and many persons who came to sympathize with him went away delighted to have met him. All my children came to love him and his advice was law to them. To me he was more than a brother; he was a very close and loving companion.

I have said that my father and uncle had gone into partnership in the seal fishery. During that time they had owned four vessels, the *Shaver, Gleaner, Emerald* and *Barbara*. The latter was a barque. Their first vessel was built by themselves. My uncle, with a crew of men, spent one winter in the Bay to cut the timbers, plank and other woodwork, and in the following fall cruised out of the Bay to Flowers Island, where she was built. My uncle superintended the building and my father made the sails. The vessel was built head towards the water, her mast was put in place and all the rigging set up before she was launched.

The morning she was launched was bitterly cold, and just before the trip was knocked away my father appeared on the scene from the sail loft and said, "Bill, if you don't put something before the stem of this vessel, she will beat her stem out on the other island." My uncle thought his own way best. In most matters he was right, but not this time. The trip was knocked away and the big ice line that my uncle trusted to stop the schooner snapped like a thread that was burnt by fire, and just as my father predicted, the vessel beat her stem out on the other island. Nothing daunted, some men were placed at the pumps, others taking on board ballast and provisions and wood for kindling. The schooner was then headed for Greenspond, where she was hove down and a new stem put in her. She sailed for the seal fishery on the 9th day of March, and arrived at St. John's on the 28th of March with a load of seals; sailed again for the second trip a few days after, arriving in St. John's on the 28th day of April with another load.

After the death of my mother, my father retired from active business and gave us, his four sons, a little fishing schooner, arranging with his brother William that his share in the *Barbara* should be transferred to us. My eldest brother was William, and our firm was known as William Kean & Brothers.

1871 marks another landmark in my history. My uncle brought in 8,100 seals, which was considered a big trip then. My uncle approached my brother and said, "I am getting old, I have two sons and it may be that you and they may not get along as well as we have. I think we had better separate," adding, "I will give you your choice, to sell or buy the *Barbara*," naming an unset price that he had placed on her. Without a moment's hesitation my brother replied, "I will sell."

With the proceeds of the sealing voyage for that year my brother bought a new vessel which was then lying at Clift's Wharf, by the name of *Peerless,* one of the best ever engaged in the seal fishery. He paid cash down for her, the purchase price being fifteen hundred pounds.[3] When I heard the news my happiness was complete. I learned afterwards from bitter experience that the day of sailing vessels in the seal fishery was over. Steam had so out-classed sailing vessels that it would be only a matter of a few years before the sailing vessel was to become a thing of the past.

I looked forward to 1872 when I would be seventeen years old and would make my first trip to the seal fishery. On the 1st of March I sailed with a crew of seventy men and bade farewell to those on the land with ringing cheers, as was the custom in those days. For three years I sailed as a common man, and after that I was promoted master of watch and later second hand[4] under my brother.

Another event took place in 1872, without mention of which my life history would be incomplete. After my mother's death my sisters married and my father was compelled to get a woman to keep house. In 1871 the woman who kept house for my father decided to forsake single blessedness and look for happiness in matrimony, which necessitated my father's looking for another housekeeper. This time he was recommended to a young woman from Cape Freels by the name of Caroline Yetman, whose parents my father had known many years before. She was written to and accepted the position. In November, 1871, my brother went to Cape Freels and brought her to Flowers Island. We soon became very friendly, and although she was seven years older than me, she was sensible enough not to allow the disparity in years spoil a good match. I was accepted.

I had just celebrated my seventeenth birthday and was not out of the control of my father, but when I approached him to ask for the hand of his housekeeper in marriage he very sensibly fell in with my wishes. On the 19th of October, 1872, the ceremony was performed at Greenspond and we became man and wife. Eleven months later our first child was born, who was destined to become probably the most popular young man in Newfoundland.

Seven other children followed in due course, making eight in all, six sons and two daughters. Two of my sons followed my profession and qualified themselves with Master Certificates of Competency. My second son became master of a steamer at the seal fishery but without a ticket. Two of my other sons are in the medical profession and practising in my old home in the North. My third son was inclined to qualify himself as a marine engineer, but unfortunately was drowned within one mile of our home at Brookfield, while skating on a pond when he was only thirteen years old.

My youngest daughter married and settled down at Brooklyn, New York. My eldest daughter married but is keeping house for me now.

In 1877 my eldest brother, William, contracted tuberculosis and was forced to give up work, and his wife and family and five children were thrown on me, besides two children belonging to my elder brother, John who died way back in the sixties. I now had eleven others besides my own family to provide for, and we all lived in one house and ate out of the same "bag and barrel" until they grew up to manhood and womanhood. Then I helped them to get houses of their own. Things were so managed that I cannot remember a single quarrel among them. My brother's girls to this very day speak of their Aunt Carrie as being a mother to them. In 1879 I removed from Flowers Island to Norton's Cove, which I afterwards called Brookfield.

From 1872 to 1882 I served at the seal fishery under my two brothers, William and Samuel, three years as a common man, the remainder as master of watch and second hand. In 1882, becoming impatient and not wishing to serve any longer under another man, I applied to Baine Johnston for the captaincy of a brigantine for the seal fishery named the *Hannie & Bennie*. My application was accepted, and sometime in December I sailed for Pool's Island to lay up until sealing time, which should commence in March.

A little over half-way down a storm overtook us, blowing away part of our canvas and forcing us to retreat to St. John's, where we had our sails repaired and then sailed again for Pool's Island a few days after. This time we succeeded, but my first venture in command was very unfortunate. That winter the ice froze on the land two miles outside the harbour where we had our vessels laid up; the steamers that were laid up in Pool's Island Inner Tickle were forced to put in through Pond Tickle, and did not sail for the seal fishery before late in March.

I encouraged my men to walk out two miles from the harbour's mouth to try to break a channel into the harbour, but the crew of the other two vessels, after one day, would not go again. We were jammed in until the 13th of April, when the ice broke up. I thereupon put to sea and was followed by my brother in the *Peerless* and my cousin in the *Barbara*, but it was too late to retrieve our lost fortunes.

The following year, in 1883, I went in command of the same vessel, but this year I laid up in my home town, Brookfield. The *Hannie & Bennie* and *Peerless*, of which I was part owner, were moored, stern on to what was known as the Peerless Rock. My father was dying of cancer. One night towards the end of December a gale of wind blew with terrific force, accompanied by a blinding snowstorm. About nine o'clock we heard a man walking along on our bridge and I felt sure he was bringing bad news. I was right in my premonition—it was a cousin of mine who came to inform me that the *Peerless* and the *Hannie & Bennie* had broken their stern moorings. The *Peerless*, he said, was swinging on her anchor, but the *Hannie & Bennie* was on the rocks. I left my home to go to the scene of the disaster amid the protests of my father, my wife and brother, who said it was madness to think of doing anything before daylight. I found they were right.

When the storm abated some two or three hundred men came to my assistance. Fortunately the *Peerless* was not damaged, and willing hands soon had her moored again. The *Hannie & Bennie* was considerably damaged, and all her ballast had to be taken out. Fortunately her store-room, where her bread and flour were, was above water. We got her off the rocks and made everything ready for heaving her down to repair damages. For eleven days, however, there was a continual gale of wind, during which time we had to keep the water out. On the twelfth day there was a complete calm, and just as we were in the act of heaving her down, my wife sent word to me that my father had taken a turn for the worse and required a doctor. Under the circumstances I could not leave my work, but engaged four men to go for the doctor.

Just as I thought, my father was past all human skill, as the doctor informed me. The next day we finished repairs, and when I told my father that the work was finished and that the *Hannie & Bennie* was tighter than she had been since I had her, he burst out crying for joy, and in a few hours breathed his last.

1 "my millionth seal" actually refers to his millionth seal pelt. The skin with the blubber attached was described as the seal pelt. The seal carcasses (except for a few for personal consumption) were left on the ice.

2 To seal on shore or from its shore was to hunt seals on the ice floes which came into the harbours and coves and to set nets in the nearby waters to catch seals. Such sealers were referred to as "landsmen."

3 Presumably Newfoundland pounds currency or about $6000.00 (U.S.).

4 The first mate was referred to as the second hand.

THE *S.S. NEWFOUNDLAND*, (INSET) CAPTAIN WESBURY KEAN, YOUNGEST SON OF CAPTAIN ABRAM KEAN. (PHOTO: CENTRE FOR NEWFOUNDLAND STUDIES ARCHIVES)

CHAPTER II

A legacy of debt—A wild gale—Schooner-building and politics—
A fantastic election—Heated personalities—The Queen of the
Fleet *sails on Friday—The father of a family goes back to*
school—Examinations and a first ship

My position at this time was by no means enviable. All the
money that we had in 1872 had been put into the *Peerless*
and was lost. The seal fishery in sailing vessels was a thing of the
past. My elder brothers were dead and the support of their
families was left to my care. My only legacy was one of debt. The
coming seal fishery might have something in store for me, but the
end of 1883 saw the last days of sailing vessels in the seal fishery,
and also the end of my career as master of a sailing vessel.

In 1884 I put in an application for the *S.S. Esquimaux* to the
Hon. Moses Monroe. He received me very kindly, but told me I
was young and had no experience with steamers and thought I
had better go for a year or two in steamers to get some
experience. I then went to Captain Joe Barbour, who kindly gave
me a berth as a bridge master.[1] For two years I served under him
at the seal fishery.

The year 1885 was destined to place my name on the map of
Newfoundland, an event which I had never thought of, even in
my wildest dreams. After coming in from the seal fishery I got
ready for the cod fishery, and on the day of starting I went to the
Funks to get some eggs for our summer, as was the custom in
those days. On Saturday evening we anchored at Rockey Bay,

11

where we intended to spend Sunday. At ten o'clock when I went on deck it was blowing a strong breeze to the eastward and most of the schooners were weighing anchor, going for a better harbour. Owing to a defective windlass and the fact that another schooner was anchored close under our stern, I trusted for the wind to drop and to allow us to ride out the storm where we were.

To my surprise, next morning there was the most terrific storm it was ever my lot to see, a gale that was henceforth to be known as the 7th of June gale. The schooner under our stern had heavy ground tackle, the race pipes split and the chains cut through the planks. She sank and turned bottom up. Fortunately, before this happened, the crew had left her in their boats and reached a harbour. Our schooner was going bowsprit under every dart, and all the other schooners had gone to a harbour. At 3 p.m. the wind showed no sign of abating, and I summoned my crew to leave the schooner and run for land to a harbour that was close by where I knew my brother was in his boat. My crew hesitated, fearing the boats would founder, but I had built the boats myself and told them they need not fear as to their stability. In due course we slipped the lines and, running for the shore, reached the harbour in safety and took refuge on board my brother's boat.

The next morning when we went on shore we saw our schooner high and dry on the rocks, a total wreck. We saved what we could out of the wreck, and one of my friends took us all in his boat and brought us home.

Two of my crew were sharemen and one was a servant. I gave the two sharemen their discharge, and with my servant and some of my brother's sons went to Wesleyville and got up an old boat that had been lying on the bottom for two years. We fixed her up at a nearby island for us to live aboard and set our traps in the water. In three weeks we trapped 180 quintals of fish.

In October I went to St. John's to get a man to build a schooner for me for the coming year. The Government in power that year was in difficulties[2] and Sir James Winter led a formidable Opposition. The Government candidate for Bonavista

12

Bay had been bitterly opposed to them in the previous winter, but changed his politics on arrival at St. John's and decided to stand for Bonavista in the Government interest. Denominationally, the candidate had to be a Methodist. The temperance question was strong, and he had to be a temperance man. Where could another man be found with these two qualifications? On my arrival in St. John's the Opposition grasped at me like drowning men clutching at straws, but as I had never given politics a thought and knew nothing about the question, I told them so. All my entreaties were of no avail. The Opposition papers took up my case, and instead of my life being the chapter of accidents that I thought it was, I was pointed to as a guiding star. I had only to give my consent and the very next day saw a flattering pen picture of myself in the Reform party paper, while the report about me in the Government paper was not so good!

I decided on a plan of campaign. My strong point would be local representation for Bonavista; it would not work in less than forty-eight hours. The Government party called out a man from Greenspond on the north side of Bonavista Bay as a local candidate also, but the opposition against the Government party was so strong that the leader of the Government became faint-hearted at almost the last moment and decided to resign if the leader of the Opposition would do otherwise, and call in an Independent man to form an amalgamated party.

This was done and Robert (afterwards Sir Robert) Thorburn took the position. Mr. Noonan and myself were chosen for Bonavista Bay to represent the Reform party and Dr. George Skelton to represent the past Government. Under this arrangement if everybody was satisfied there was to be no election, only a nomination. As nomination day was drawing near we took on board a cask of porter, some biscuits and cheese and made a tour around the Bay to visit our friends, planning to reach Bonavista the night before nomination.

We carried out our plans to the letter, arriving in Bonavista at 9 p.m. This was before the days of the telegraph, and we had heard nothing from the outside world. Much to our surprise a boat came up from the shore and informed us that there was to be an election in Bonavista Bay, that A. B. Morine, a member of the Government party, who was not satisfied with amalgamation, had kicked over the traces and was standing on an Independent ticket. Frederick White of Greenspond was chosen by the Government party to offset me on the other side. My two colleagues were much older than me, and the news was a bombshell to them. Next day was nomination day. We had canvassed the Bay, telling the people that we were the chosen three and that there was to be no election. Now we had to retrace our steps and tell them a very different story.

Next day we were all duly nominated, and that night our party hired the hall and had a public meeting. Mr. Morine took his place in the hall, and when the meeting commenced, asked for permission to come upon the platform. My two colleagues began talking to the chairman in an undertone; I overheard the conversation and found that they were planning to prevent Morine from coming upon the platform. I observed that it was not only discourteous but cowardly, and that nothing we could do in Bonavista would damn us so much politically as refusing Morine a seat on the platform. This argument prevailed, and Morine came up amid the clapping of hands and the cheers of his supporters. On reaching the platform, he made his bow to the chairman and said, "Ladies and gentlemen, I don't think you could do a better thing than return Mr. Kean as one of your representatives. I question if that's not more than Kean will say for me."

Two weeks before I had met Morine at Greenspond, and that very day I received a message from headquarters which said: "You will meet Morine in Greenspond soon. Tell the people to reject him as a traitor, an enemy and a spy." When some of Morine's friends tried to make a disturbance at our meeting I said, "I know nothing of this man Morine, but I got a message from St. John's today and this is what it says," and I read the message. To this Morine replied that he did not object to me as much as the party which concocted that message. Whatever other opinions we may have formed of him, I think that we were unanimous on one point, and that was that he was a very talented speaker, and as far as Newfoundland politics were concerned he knew it all from A to Z. The rest of us were like so many midgets in his hands.

He was not only a good speaker but a man of great discernment and tact. I had just made my maiden speech in Bonavista. I was very green in politics but I had some experience in public speaking, and once on my feet it was not easy to shake me. From start to finish, every point I scored was greeted with cheers that shook the building. Morine saw at a glance that as far as Bonavista was concerned I would be elected, as subsequent events proved. When the votes were counted in Bonavista proper, I led and Morine came next, but over the whole Bay, Morine lost ground. When the state of the poll was declared, Noonan, White and I were elected, and Morine and Dr. Skelton defeated.

On getting back to St. John's, Morine published a letter in one of the papers in which he pilloried the party with which I was associated but "thanked heaven" that I was elected.

Our opposition in these first political battles lessened as we grew to know each other better, for we looked for the good in each other rather than for the faults. For the last thirty years we have been the best of friends. And when His Majesty the King conferred his birthday honour upon me, one of the first foreign messages I received was from Sir A. B. Morine, together with most cordial letters from himself and his son.

1886 was the dawn of a new epoch for me. At the appointed time I took my seat in the Legislative Hall of my country and thought in terms of State. For a time, at least, the seal fishery, which had hitherto been the idol of my heart, had now to be kept in the background. The sessional pay at that time was but $300 for the session, out of which I had to pay board and lodging from January until May. In 1885 I had engaged Samuel Mitchem of

15

Green's Harbour to build me a new schooner to take the place of the *E. Morine,* which I had lost in Rockey [sic] Bay in the 7th of June gale. When she was ready to launch I took my crew and went from St. John's to Green's Harbour to see the launch and to take charge of her for the coming cod fishery. We arrived at Green's Harbour on a Friday, very much to the disappointment of the master builder, who never believed in starting any new enterprise on a Friday, and begged me not to launch her until the next day. Superstition and luck were two things I could never believe in, and I soon told him so. Consequently I ordered him to launch her the first thing after breakfast. He did so, and she was called the *Queen of the Fleet.*

Owing to the necessary fixing up in a new vessel we were late in starting, and when we arrived at the Wadman Islands the other schooners reported that they had no fish, that they had their traps broken up and were undergoing repairs. I set my traps right away and in one week trapped more fish than any two vessels there. We went back home and landed our shore fish and refitted for Labrador, where we loaded her again. The second year I was in her was known as the summer of scarcity on the Labrador; lots of schooners got no more than fifty quintals for their summer. On the 3rd day of September I came out of Siglet Bay in the *Queen of the Fleet,* log-loaded with fish—my main deck only two inches from the water. So much for Friday as an unlucky day!

In 1887, in Christmas week, I came to St. John's from the North with my family and took a house on Military Road. I sent my children to the Methodist College, for I was determined that they should not suffer for want of an education. I thought I could see in the not so far distant future a time when every man would be required to have a Certificate of Competency before he would be allowed to take charge of life and property.

I approached Sir Robert Thorburn and told him that I intended to go to school and qualify myself for a Master's Certificate. He greatly approved of my action, and told me that if he ever wanted a master he would recommend me. When school commenced after Christmas I started every morning for school with my children, they going to the Methodist College and I to Mr. Francis Doyle, who taught navigation. Sometime during the winter the Hon. Edward White invited Mr. F. White, the member for Bonavista Bay, and myself to tea in his home on the South Side, and during the conversation he informed me that Messrs. Harvey had consulted him about two composite boats they were building for Government mail boats, adding that the *Plover* and *Curlew* were too small for the work, but one of them might be suitable for the Labrador service. I kept my own counsel but wrote to my friend Captain Robert Gosse of Spaniard's Bay, John Sparkes of Bay Roberts, and others, and told them I intended to apply for the Labrador boat for the coming summer, requesting their support. This each one promised to give.

On the 22nd of May, 1888, I passed my examination and was awarded a Certificate of Competency. In due course the *Conscript* and *Volunteer* came on the scene and Harvey's secured the contract. Captain Pat Delaney, who was master of the *Curlew* in Bowrings' employ, resigned to take charge of the *Volunteer.* As soon as I heard this I went to the Hon. Charles Bowring, who was then head of the firm of Bowring, and put in my application for the *Curlew.* He, however, advised me to go with Captain Delaney on one trip to the west coast to learn the ways of the ship, so that within a month of securing my certificate I got my first ship, the *Curlew,* on the Labrador Mail Service.

Just before the House closed in 1888 Mr. Walter Baine Grieve walked down to my seat and said to me, "If you could get a steamer for the seal fishery would you take her?" I replied, "Would a duck swim?" "Well," he replied, "I have reason to believe that the *Wolf* will go north the next spring. You had better see Sir Robert yourself." Sir Robert was sitting in his seat but not engaged at any particular business as the House was in Committee on some minor matter. I went straight up to him and told him what I had heard, at the same time putting in my verbal application. He received my application very favourably, told me that he owned half of the *Wolf* himself and that I could rely on his support. The appointment of masters for the coming year did not take place until the Director's meeting, which generally took place about September. Like Mary of old, I kept all these sayings and pondered them over in my heart. But my aspirations were aroused—the major ambition of my life was to command a steamer to the seal fishery. I had worked and planned with that object in view and fortune seemed against me at every turn I took; every time I put in an application and was refused seemed to dampen my spirits and make life unbearable. I had never thought of politics, and, without any effort of my own, I was pitchforked into a position which I had neither sought after nor desired. For three years I had laboured at politics, looking towards the future and wondering what there was in store for me.

It is only fair to say, however, that I became very much interested in politics, and have no doubt that if I had put the same energy into politics as I had put in at the seal fishery, I might today find myself in the same position as many another ex-Prime Minister in this country. They, like Samson of old, have had the strength taken from them, and rightly or wrongly have been blamed for their share of the waste and extravagance which brought this country to the verge of bankruptcy and reduced it to the status of a Crown Colony. Fate, however, decreed otherwise.

---

1 The bridge master relayed instructions to the men at the helm.

2 Premier Whiteway's government had fallen over the results of the trials held after the Harbour Grace riot of December, 1883. The election of 1885 was won by the Reform Party under Robert Thorburn who promised "no amalgamation with Roman Catholics."

CHAPTER III

Winter in the Wolf—*A snowstorm*—*26,000 whitecoats*—*Family vicissitudes*—*The new school*—*Leaving Flowers Island*

Meanwhile I had entered into a verbal partnership with my nephew, Jacob Kean (who now commands the *Prospero*). We dealt with Allan Goodridge & Sons, presided over by Frederick Goodridge, who long before this had won for himself the title "The Rupert of Debate." On my taking charge of the *Curlew* I had Jacob Kean appointed master of the *Queen of the Fleet*. In the course of time I took up my position as master of the *S.S. Curlew* on the Labrador Mail Service, and after finishing that work, I was ordered to go to Trinity and "swop" steamers with Captain Frank Ash, who was in charge of the *Falcon* doing mail service in Trinity Bay. The *Falcon* was owned by the same firm as the *Curlew,* and as the latter was more suitable for the mail service than the *Falcon,* I was asked to hand over the *Curlew* to Captain Ash and to take the *Falcon* for the foreign trade.

My first trip in the *Falcon* from Trinity to South Sydney and back to St. John's was said to have been the quickest on record. We brought a load of coal[1] to the dock, and when I went on board to my dinner the mate, who was Captain Charlie Carter (father of Captain Sandy Carter of the *S.S. Earl of Devon*) said to me, "Job Brothers have been inquiring for you all the morning; I don't know if they have a steamer to offer you for the spring or not."

After dinner I made a bee-line for Jobs' office, and Mr. George Hutchings said, "Messrs. Job Brothers intend sending the

Hector north this spring for the seal fishery, and I want to know if you could recommend a master, or whether perhaps you would go in her yourself." This was now in October or November, and I had not heard a word from Sir Robert Thorburn. I said, "I will give you the names of five men and I will include my own name, and if you make a choice of one of the others, you and I will not be worse friends." He replied, "Well, that's more than fair." The names I submitted were those of Benjamin Kean, William Barbour, George Barbour, Jacob Winsor, John Winsor and myself.

I then went to Sir Robert Thorburn and told him what I had done. He pointed out that the *Wolf* was a much better ship than the *Hector.* "Yes," I replied, "and if you will offer me the *Wolf* I will withdraw from the *Hector.*" "Well," he said, "all the Directors are in town, and I think I can give you an answer by five o'clock this evening." I asked him who the shareholders were, and two of those named were John McNeal and the Hon. Moses Monroe. I went straight to McMurdos and met Moses Monroe there. I never saw two men so much interested in another man's welfare as these were in mine. At 5 p.m. I was appointed master of the *S.S. Wolf* for the coming seal fishery, and went at once to Mr. Hutchings and told him that he could withdraw my name from the *Hector.* Captain Ben Kean, the first man I had recommended, was appointed master of that ship.

On New Year's Day, 1889, I arrived in the *Wolf* at Pool's Island, one hundred miles north of St. John's, to lay up for the seal fishery, which was to commence in March. As was the custom in those days, many of my friends congratulated me on what they considered a good New Year's gift. It was beyond doubt that any man in charge of a ship the size of the *Wolf,* if he were fortunate, had the best paying business. If he were not fortunate, he would not hold the job long. I was in a good position for making money; I was also in a good way to spend it, for three days after my arrival in Pool's Island we had another increase in the family, this time my youngest son.

During the winter one of my friends took me into his confidence and said, "Your best plan is to keep in the wake of some of those captains who never miss the seals—Joe Barbour, for example. If you can only get into the seals you will be bound to get your share." That year the sailing date came on Sunday, and the law provided that when the sailing date came on this day the steamers could sail on Saturday. Consequently, we all got ready to sail on Saturday, but the wind had packed the ice on land and there was no water except out to Pool's Island Point. All the steamers weighed anchor and went and stuck in the ice near the point of the island. I, being the hindermost, did not sail until the afternoon, and when I left I went on the mail top and noticed a crack in the ice which, I decided, was the ice moving off.

I headed for the crack, and to my delight and surprise the *Wolf* commenced to make headway, leaving the other seven ships in the rear. What was I to do? Should I take the advice of my friend and wait until some other man got ahead, or steer my own course? I was not long in choosing. I sent word to the engine-room to put on all steam, and it was not long before the distance between us and the hinder ship grew wider and wider. It became thick with snow, and we got out of sight of the hinder ships.

About 11 a.m. we sighted another ship ahead which turned out to be the *S.S. Aurora*, Captain McKay, from St. John's, who had got ahead of us during Saturday, when we were icebound in Pool's Island. We caught up on him, and by Monday he was in our wake and held our wake until noon, when it got thick and we lost sight of him. About 4 p.m. Monday afternoon in a thick snowstorm we ran into a patch of whitecoats.[2] Next morning the work commenced in dead earnest, and on March 20th we arrived in St. John's, making the round trip from Pool's Island to St. John's in eleven days, being the quickest trip on record. Total number of seals being 26,912. We went out on a second trip and arrived back to St. John's on the 23rd of April with 4,561 seals, mostly old.

I have pointed out elsewhere that I had entered into a verbal agreement with my nephew, Jacob Kean. I mentioned also that he had been appointed master of the *Queen of the Fleet* and dealt with Allan Goodridge & Sons. A debt was contracted there in my name for which I was held responsible. Knowing that it was hopeless to dicker about it, I went to Goodridge & Sons and paid $1,300, this being the total amount of the liability. I then handed over to Jacob Kean and his brothers and sisters my share of the *Queen of the Fleet* and helped to build them a house. We separated....

My elder brother's son, Job, who is so well known as Captain Job Kean, stayed with me until he married. He had left me a year before, but his first child was born while he and his wife were living in my house. The wives of my deceased brothers had married a second time, but did not take any of their children with them. My nieces all married and made good matches for themselves. Captain Job Kean was second hand with me for a number of years and afterwards became master at the seal fishery and commanded the *S.S. Leopard*, the *S.S. Erik* and *S.S. Diana*. Captain Jacob Kean gave up the fishing business and entered into the Coastal trade. He became very friendly with the Hon. Samuel Blandford, who was Reid's Superintendent of Shipping, and soon became master of one of the Coastal boats. When Captain Blandford became sick while he was master of the *Virginia Lake,* Jacob Kean, at his recommendation, became master of the *Virginia Lake.* Later he had charge of nine more different ships. Edwin Kean, who was a brother of Jacob Kean, distinguished himself as a fish-killer and was for two years master of the *S.S. Iceland* at the seal fishery. The second year, however, he lost her and did not command another.

I had now reached a stage in my life's history when I had relieved myself of all responsibility for my brothers' children. I have shown also how each of my brothers' sons became a useful citizen and played his part in the country's business. Only one of them failed to distinguish himself and he, through ill-health, died young.

To return to the question of education. When I came back from school I was the only one on the two islands who could read or write. The parents became alarmed as never before, and began to say, "Why cannot we get a school here for children?" Although I was not out of my teens I interested the Methodist Church, of which I was a member, and succeeded in securing a teacher. The first teacher was Miss Lucrecia Oakley from Greenspond, who afterwards became the wife of Captain George Barbour. The next teacher was Miss Virtue Hann, who afterwards became the wife of Captain Job Kean. Both of these teachers did good service and the parents responded magnificently. The girls, of course, received most benefit, as the fathers of the boys did not set sufficient value on education to keep their boys at school when fish could be caught. The school at Flowers Island had a short life.

I could not get fish in a small boat as my father had done, but had to get a large schooner and go to Labrador as others were doing these days. I soon found that Flowers Island could not afford a harbour for a schooner of that size, and moved to a place called Norton's Cove, which I afterwards named Brookfield. I moved to Brookfield in 1879, and in a few years every other family followed. For the last thirty years Flowers Island has provided a place for wild flowers to grow and birds to build their nests and hatch their young as nature and grace intended. Truly a vastly different opinion from that which I held when I was eight years old! My father was bitterly opposed to my leaving Flowers Island, but less than a year later he was living at Brookfield. One day he said to me, "What a fool I was to spend all my days at Flowers Island!"

1 Newfoundland imported considerable quantities of coal from Sydney, Nova Scotia.

2 Young harp seals.

LANDING PELTS

SNAPPED UNAWARES AFTER LONG WAITING

CHAPTER IV

The loss of the Wolf—*Cabinet Minister—The move to St. John's—The '98 Contract—Politics and seals*

We now return to 1889. The party with which I had been associated had come into power in 1885 with a sweeping majority. In the election of 1889 I was taking no part. I had a steamer for the seal fishery, and as I would be away during the legislative session and did not think it would be fair to continue, I withdrew from the contest, with the result that every member of our victorious party in 1885 came back.[1] Meanwhile, I was pursuing the even tenor of my ways, and from 1889 to 1895 brought to port in the *Wolf* 155,579 seals, or an average of 22,225 seals, the best average ever made up to that time.

In 1896 I lost the *Wolf* eight miles from Fogo Harbour, where we had to walk on shore. On reaching land, I wired to the owners: "I am sorry to inform you I lost your fine ship. No one to be blamed but myself; it was an error of judgment on my part." The following year I commanded the *S.S. Hope* and made one of the worst years I ever made from the time I commanded a steamer.

The period 1889 to 1897 proved to be a chapter of accidents as far as governments were concerned. The Government elected in 1889 had been elected under the Ballot Act[2] and was unseated for bribery and corruption. On the 8th of July, 1892, St. John's was swept by fire, almost the whole of the east end being destroyed. In 1894 we had the bank crash, and in seven years we

25

had no less than four Prime Ministers. The legislature no longer sat in winter, but in late spring or summer.

In 1897 Sir James Winter led the Opposition and I was asked to stand for the district of Bay de Verde, a district that was always so evenly divided that the victorious party never had a big majority. I consented to stand, and when the poll was declared I had the largest majority ever polled up to that time. My colleague was also elected. Sir James Winter offered me a seat in his Cabinet, which I accepted. During that session we created a Department of Marine and Fisheries for the first time, and I was appointed Acting Minister of Marine and Fisheries. According to law I had to vacate that position in six months. When the term had expired, Mr. Morine approached me and said, "Kean, you have made your mark in the seal fishery; why don't you resign the seal fishery and hold on to the Minister of Marine and Fisheries?" My reply was, "Morine, you have not got enough money in the Government chest to purchase me from the seal fishery."

After 1889 I went into a mercantile business, north at Brookfield, and was the owner of several schooners, which were doing well. My sons were looking after the business. I was Minister of Marine and Fisheries and had to reside at St. John's. Already we had gone to and fro from St. John's to Brookfield three or four times; I was tired of moving and bought a house on Prescott Street, St. John's, and settled down, leaving my old home in Brookfield to my children.

In 1898 I took charge of the *Aurora* from Bowring Brothers. In this ship I had remarkable good fortune, bringing to port 204,517 seals in eight years; an average of 25,564 seals per spring.

In 1898 our Government passed what was known as the '98 Contract, in which we cancelled the Coastal contract under Harvey's and gave Reid's the right to put on Bay boats to connect with the railway all around the island.[3] I was sent to Scotland to superintend the plan of these boats on behalf of the Government.

Robert Bond (who afterwards became Sir Robert) was leader of the Opposition, and bitterly opposed the so-called '98 Contract. Two years after our Government came into power, and while some of our supporters were out of the country, the House was opened for a short session to pass some measure relating to the French Shore question. The leader of the Opposition proceeded to move a vote of no confidence. Notwithstanding the fact that Sir James Winter was promised the entire support of his party, three of his supporters crossed the floor, voted with the Opposition and defeated the Government. A General Election followed. The Opposition had promised a complete reform in the '98 Contract, maintaining that our Government had sold the country to the Reids, and that even our graveyards were not safe.

The propaganda carried conviction to the majority of the people, and Bond and his party swept the country and came back with a smashing majority. Much to the disgust of their supporters, very few changes were made in the '98 Contract. Not a solitary boat of the Reids' was diverted from her course, but more were added on. Mr. Bond, the leader of the Government, thereupon entered into an agreement with Sir Robert Reid that if he would hand back to the Crown some of the Crown land that was given to him under the '98 Contract, the Government would pay them back cash at a price that would be determined by an impartial tribunal. This was accepted by Sir Robert Reid. In due course a settlement was reached; the land was handed back to the Crown, and Sir Robert Reid was paid $800,000. Sir Robert acknowledged to a friend of mine that the period between his entering into the agreement with the Government and his obtaining the money was the most anxious time of his life, for he had already learned by bitter experience that all is not gold that glitters, i.e. that the land that he possessed was not as valuable as he at first thought when he entered into the '98 Contract, as subsequent events proved.

Apart from paying Reid for the land which the '98 Contract gave him, the Government of Sir Robert Bond advertised for tenders for two boats to ply on the outside in addition to the six or seven steamers which were given the Reids under the '98 Contract. The Bowrings tendered and were awarded the contract. By this time my eldest son, J.W., had made quite a name for himself, already having charge of the Government yacht *Fiona* and having made two or three trips around the island, once with Sir John Branston and others in connection with the settlement of the French question, and once with the Judges of the Supreme Court. Through no fault of his own he was turned out of his job by a change of Government. Such, I regret to note, were the miserable tactics of Newfoundland politics at that time.

When I read that the Bowrings were awarded the contract I went to Sir Edgar Bowring and put in an application for my son, J.W., for one of the boats. He replied, "No, Captain, I think Joe is too young. We want a man of more prestige, but I think you could fill the position and Joe could go with you as mate. No doubt Joe's time will come later. Your other sons can look after the business, and if you say so we will supply them." As I have pointed out, I had charge of the Labrador Mail and Passenger Service and was fascinated by the work. I told Sir Edgar Bowring that I would consult the boys and give him an answer the following day. I took Joe into my confidence and told him of my interview with Sir Edgar Bowring. Joe agreed, and the next morning I accepted Sir Edgar's offer, was appointed master of the *S.S. Portia*, and in 1904 went with my son Joe and the rest of the crew to Scotland to bring out the *Portia* for the Northern Service of Newfoundland.

Here again fortune came to me from an unexpected quarter. I was placed in a good position for the whole summer as well as for the seal fishery in the spring. This I could never have done had not our party been defeated. While I was at Port Glasgow the *Prospero,* which was intended for the west coast, was launched. A small platform was built at the bow for Lady William Bowring to stand on the perform the christening, and I was invited to stand by her side. When the trip was knocked away, Lady Bowring smashed the bottle against her bow and called her *Prospero*. Before she touched the water she was going 15 or 20 knots; on reaching the water her stern rose and her head went down. Lady Bowring turned to me. "I declare, Captain Kean," she said, "she bowed like a lady."

In due time the *Prospero* arrived and was given in charge of Captain Thomas Fitzpatrick of Placentia. After two years we "swopped" boats for reasons which need not be explained here. I took over the *Prospero* and Captain Fitzpatrick took the *Portia*.

In 1910 Captain Fitzpatrick resigned from the *Portia* and took charge of the Customs of Placentia, and my son, J. W. Kean, was promoted master of the *S.S. Portia* on the south-west coast, thereby fulfilling the words of Sir Edgar Bowring, "Joe's time will come." From 1904 to 1914 nothing out of the ordinary in my life took place except that very large steel ships had been engaged at the seal fishery, and I had been placed in command of two of them. In 1910 and 1916 I had brought in the largest number and the largest weight ever brought in during the world's history, which record held good until 1933, when it was beaten by the *Imogene* and *Ungave*. It is only fair to say, however, that I was competing against nineteen ships and that they were competing against six.

From 1904 to 1914 three of my sons had been promoted to master ships at the seal fishery, which was due in some measure, perhaps, to the success which had attended my efforts in that industry. Their names are J. W. Kean, Nathan Kean and Westbury B. Kean. Each served under me previously as common hand, master watch and second hand.

1 This is unclear. In the 1889 election Robert Thorburn's party lost and William Whiteway's Liberal Party returned to office.

2 Thorburn's government had passed legislation which brought in the secret ballot and which defined certain campaign practices as bribery, treating and corruption and set penalties for those convicted of such illegalities.

3 Robert Reid was given many concessions and the agreement was very unpopular in the colony as a whole.

S.S. Nascopie

S.S. Wolf

CHAPTER V

Death on the ice—A blinding snowstorm—A political vendetta—
Mud-slinging and apologies

That part of my history which took place in 1914 and the succeeding years is one which I would willingly forget, but painful recollection must be sacrificed on the altar of truth. Through no fault of my own I was subjected to the most bitter attack launched on any man in this or any other country.

My son, who was in command of the *S.S. Newfoundland*, had his crew caught out on the ice one night, and seventy-three of his crew perished.[1] These men were on board my ship at noon and I gave them a dinner, and during the time they were eating their dinner I steamed to a small spot of seals and put them down among the seals and then steamed towards my own men. At that time it was calm, but the sky was overcast. At 3 p.m. a sudden gale sprang up with a blinding snowstorm. My first duty was to look after my own crew, and as soon as I got them on board I made tracks for the *Newfoundland's* crew, but as soon as the ice touched the land my ship was unable to move. I put on all my lights and kept my whistle blowing until I was fully convinced that the crew had reached their own ship. Unfortunately, the Newfoundland had no wireless, but even if she had, the accident could not have been averted.

This attack was made by the man who afterwards became Sir William Coaker, and who blamed me for the loss of these men.

On the 4th of August that year war broke our between Germany and England, and in September, 1914, when I went to Sir

Edgar Bowring to put in my application for the *Stephano* for the coming spring, Sir Edgar said, "I am afraid your ship, the *Stephano,* owing to the war, will not prosecute the seal fishery. I am not thinking about you, however, but about Joe, for whichever of the two ships go, you will have to go in her."

Almost every day the *Mail and Advocate* (the Union paper) made charges against me, which I persistently denied. Finally they accused me of having taken, twenty-six years ago, two barrels of beef and pork from the ship's stores and of using it myself, putting inferior food in its place. Further, that in the investigation of the *Newfoundland* disaster, I had perjured myself and given a false oath. I at once engaged Mr. Warren, a prominent lawyer (who afterwards became Judge Warren) to institute legal proceedings against Coaker for defamation of character, claiming $20,000 damages. Coaker's paper, the *Advocate,* kept up a bombardment of charges until the climax was reached.

The *Advocate* announced that petitions were being signed all over the country to the effect that I was never to take charge of another ship to the seal fishery. To this I paid little or no attention until one day the *Advocate* announced in great headlines that Bowring's had decided that I was not to command a ship for the coming spring, and expressed regret at the unfortunate circumstances which had led up to this. They were doing their best to damn me with their faint praise.

I went immediately to Bowring's office and found the late John Munn (who was at that time head of Bowrings' firm in St. John's) white with indignation. When I asked him for the news for my information, he handed me the message from their London office, which read, "Owing to the war, the *Stephano* will not prosecute the seal fishery and Captain Abram Kean will not go to the seal fishery the coming spring." He then handed me a document to read, which ran more or less as follows: "Are you going to permit your legally appointed Directors to do your business for you or are we to be dictated to by any individual who comes your way? Captain Abram Kean has an agreement from Sir

Edgar so far back as September that whichever of the two ships goes to the seal fishery he will command her."

This happened on Saturday afternoon. Saturday night was the first night I lost a moment's sleep over all the accusations which, from time to time, had been levelled against me, and on Sunday afternoon I went to Mr. Eric Bowring to talk matters over with him and try to get their London office to stay any hasty proceedings until they had heard from me. When the girl mentioned my name I saw Mr. Eric racing down the steps, his face beaming. There was a paper in his hand. It was a note from their London office and read: "We knew nothing of the agreement between Sir Edgar and Captain Kean. Captain Kean is appointed master of the *Florizel* the coming spring."

The two cases I had pending in the Supreme Court for defamation of character against Coaker were still unsettled, and one day when I came home to my dinner I found a letter from the Prime Minister, Sir Edward Morris (now Lord Morris), asking me if I would meet him at his office at 3 p.m. Sharp on time I appeared, not having the slightest knowledge of what my mission was. To my great surprise he said, "Mr. Coaker has filed petitions against seven members of my party for bribery and corruption, and one can never tell what will happen with a jury. If these men are unseated my Government may be defeated. Coaker has asked me to get you to accept an apology with those cases you have pending against him in the Supreme Court and he will withdraw the petitions which he has against the members of my party."

He assured me that he would see that it would be a most abject apology. I replied, "Sir Edward, that would be a very fine thing for your party and no doubt a good thing for you. But where do I come in? This man already has turned some of the best friends I have in this country against me, making charges of the foulest nature, and if I accept an apology from him, all the water in the ocean will never wash me clean in the eyes of the people." Sir Edward Morris said, "Well, if that's the stand you are going to take, then the Supreme Court will have to speak." I went direct to Warren's office and said to him, "Sir Edward sent for me. What do you think it was about?" He replied, "I suppose he wanted you to accept an apology from Coaker." I said, "Did you know anything about it?" Laughing, he said, "They have been after me this last two months," and added, "I would advise you to see Furlong." He was the second lawyer I had engaged. When I interviewed Furlong he said, "Well, Captain, I believe you are entirely innocent, but nothing is more uncertain than the verdict of a jury and a dog-fight. If you accept the apology, in my opinion, it will kill Coaker better than any other thing." Mr. Morine was a great friend of mine but he was Coaker's lawyer also. He advised me to accept an apology, saying that it would only be a nine days' talk. He added that he had been eating crow almost every day since he came to the country.[2]

Beaten at every turn, I asked Furlong to give me copies of the apology that they were prepared to make by ten o'clock next morning. I wended my way homewards, half beaten and very discouraged. Sharp at 10 a.m. next morning I was at Mr. Furlong's office. He was speaking over the telephone and I overheard him say as I opened the door, "Well, you know, Morine, I don't think the Captain will be satisfied." On seeing me, he put his hand over the mouthpiece of the phone and said, "Captain, Mr. Morine tells me Coaker says he will give you an apology for the first case" (the accusation of theft), "but you have to drop the other case" [perjury]. "If that's what he says," I replied, "you can tell Morine I will not accept either. You go ahead and I will trust to the righteousness of my cause."

By four o'clock that evening I had two apologies in my pocket, but I would accept neither. We were to sail on the 13th of March. My first case was coming before Court on the 11th of March. My lawyer addressed the jury in due course—it was the most eloquent address I ever listened to. The jury retired and in a short time returned with a verdict in my favour for $500.

Some of my crew approached me and asked me if I needed a bodyguard next morning to accompany me to the ship. I thanked them, but did not think it was necessary. Next morning, the day of sailing, I left my home at 7 a.m. and walked alone to my ship, which was moored to Harvey's Wharf, and as I walked through, the crowd of men lifted their caps and wished me, "Good morning" as they always had done, which I acknowledged. Mine was the first ship that steamed through the Narrows that year for the seal fishery. It is only fair, however, to say that Coaker was perhaps deceived by many who had concocted vile stories about me. To my mind a man of his intelligence should have exercised better judgment than to have believed them.

I must add that not all union men took part in the war that was waged against me, and many of the men who took a foremost part against me have gone down to the vile dust from which they had sprung, unwept, unhonoured and unsung. Others sought forgiveness on their deathbeds. I answered that they not only had my forgiveness but my sincere sympathy for being cajoled and fooled as they were.

My second case for perjury was tried in the fall session of the Supreme Court. The Defence made no effort to prove their case, and in a very short time the jury brought in a verdict in my favour for $1,800, the largest award ever made for a similar case in our Courts. The Defence appealed on the plea that I did not want money but wanted justice. Another jury was appointed and gave a verdict in my favour for $100, and when one of my friends approached the foreman of the jury and told him I had to give all that to my lawyer, he declared the did not know I had to pay my lawyer but thought the other party had to pay. Another proof of the frequency with which the cause of justice may be frustrated by an incompetent jury.

When the appointed time of sailing came [i.e. 1916], the different ships left amid the tooting of whistles and the ringing cheers of thousands of spectators on the land. Not a gun was fired, not a blow was struck, and, best of all, I was leading the van. Coaker and his followers had sown to the wind; they were now reaping the whirlwind.

1 The final figure was seventy-eight (78).

2 Morine was from Nova Scotia.

ANXIOUS RELATIVES AND FRIENDS AWAIT THE ARRIVAL OF THE *S.S. NEWFOUNDLAND* IN ST. JOHN'S, FOLLOWING THE GREAT SEALING DISASTER OF 1914. (PHOTO: CENTRE FOR NEWFOUNDLAND STUDIES ARCHIVES)

CHAPTER VI

*Birth of the Little Stephano Company—Death of my eldest son—
Women in business—A chapter of accidents—A bankrupt
insurance company—"Politics makes strange bedfellows"—
Public scandals—Backdoor politics*

The year 1917 opens up another chapter in my life's history utterly different from anything I had yet experienced. My son, W.B. Kean, had developed a desire for a seafaring life. Owing to the war, freights had gone up, surpassing anything for the last hundred years since Great Britain was at war with her colonies in British North America. When I came in from the ice a Nova Scotian schooner was lying at Bowrings' Wharf by the name of the *Marguerite*. She was about 130 tons, her master was John B. Welkie, with a $3,000 charter, and she was for sale for $8,000, including the charter. I bought her and sent her across with a load of fish, my son, W.B., going supercargo [i.e. passenger].

They made a quick trip. My son qualified himself in navigation and on the second trip went as master. He made two other trips that year, and on the third, late in November, lost her rudder and had to abandon her. Fortunately, he and his crew were taken off by a passing steamer and brought here and landed. While discharging cargo on the other side, W.B. had come in contact with captains of three-masted schooners from the west coast, who showed him the advantages of three-masted schooners over two-masted schooners like the *Marguerite*. We talked three-masted schooners from morn till night. The *Marguerite* had not been a bad paying proposition. I had promised Wes when he had paid me back the money I paid for her, that the *Marguerite* would be his. He ran her seven months, and when she was lost I was paid the money I paid for her out of her insurance, and Wes was in credit to the extent of $7,000. Before Christmas of that year I had entered into a contract with a firm in Nova Scotia to build me a three-masted schooner of about 150 tons which we named *Little Stephano*. I had previously had charge of the Red Cross Line *Stephano* at the seal fishery and was very fond of her. She had been torpedoed by a German submarine off Nantucket Lightship. I intended to commemorate her by a line of schooners which I planned to put in the foreign service since, while the war lasted, there seemed to be no better investment.

Two of my sons had qualified as doctors and were serving in the Great War. I wrote to them and told them of my intention of building some schooners for the foreign trade and asked them to form part of a company, the membership of which I proposed to limit to the family. They consented, and we formed a company known as the Little Stephano Company with a paid-up capital stock of $50,000.

In due course the *Little Stephano* was launched, and under the captaincy of my son, Captain W. B. Kean, proved a great success. He did not command her long before he discovered that we had made a mistake in not building her larger, saying that she should have been 250 tons instead of 150. Before we had been running the *Little Stephano* for six months I had the keel of another schooner laid, which was to cost us $50,000. Our capital stock was then increased to $75,000,. Unfortunately, after we had laid the keel of our second vessel (which was afterwards named the *Cecil Jr.*), and after I had paid $7,000 on her construction, circumstances arose which almost made me wish I had never been born.

My son, J. W. Kean, who had previously been master of the *Florizel* at the seal fishery, had been put out of command owing to the war, when I was appointed master of his ship. He now applied to Farquhar & Company for the command of the S.S. *Sable Island*.

He was appointed master of that ship for the 1918 seal fishery. The owners promised to send the *Sable Island* to Newfoundland in time for the coming spring, and Joe, thinking he would enjoy a trip to Halifax, embarked on the ill-fated *Florizel* on Saturday night and lost his life next morning, when that ship ran on shore at Cappahayden, fifteen miles north-east of Cape Race. On hearing the news my feelings can be better imagined than described. He was my eldest son and had considerable experience in the business of shipping, which we had just gone into, and into which I had invested every dollar I had made. He had made a tour twice around the island in the *S.S. Fiona*, besides being master of the *Portia* on the south-west coast; he had made a host of friends and was deservedly popular. The sealers were just about to sail, and the sailing date was put back for the funeral so that the crews of the different ships could attend. The crew that had been engaged under him in the *Sable Island* were to go in that ship under the command of another man.

The funeral was beyond all doubt the largest ever seen in Newfoundland; it was not only impressive, it was heart-rending. I looked at it from every angle, but insurmountable difficulties seemed to be blocking the way. One thing I felt I could not afford to do: I could not afford to be a coward. Already Joe had bought a piece of land and laid the foundation of a house which, in all, cost him $2,700, and now that he was gone the house was far too large for his widow and two small children. If it were put up for sale, someone would want to acquire it as a bargain, and at the expense of his wife and children. I decided to buy it and hand back to the widow and children the price he had paid for it. We allowed the widow to retain the shares he had in the Little Stephano Company and paid her Director's fees. I gave the two daughters $500 each in the Little Stephano Company.

The morning after the funeral I left for the seal fishery, carrying with me through the Narrows the heaviest burden I ever bore. After coming from the seal fishery I went to the manager of the Royal Bank of Canada, Mr. Mitchell, to discuss with him whether or not to continue the building of the new schooner. Already I had paid $7,000 for her construction, and very soon I would be called upon to pay another instalment. After some consultation Mr. Mitchell (the manager) said, "Well, Captain, we cannot live by the dead, we have got to carry on." She was launched in September, and in charge of Wes proved a great success. In less than three years we had both vessels paid for and the Little Stephano Company had $14,000 to its credit in the bank.

1919 marked a landmark both in my history and in that of the Little Stephano Company. My son, W.B., who had been master of sailing vessels long enough to qualify for a Certificate of Competence as master, had a still greater desire to become a master of a steam, rather than a sailing, vessel. He studied navigation and passed a very successful examination as master.

There was to be a General Election in Newfoundland that year, and the leader of the Government, Sir Michael Cashin, approached me and asked me if I would stand for the district of St. Barbe. At that time I was master of the Coastal boat *S.S. Prospero*, and he promised me if I would consent they would place my son, W.B., in charge of that vessel. I accepted the offer and my son, W.B., was placed in command of the *Prospero*. When the poll was declared Sir Michael Cashin's party was defeated, and I was one of the victims.[1]

Shortly after the election we called a meeting of the shareholders of the Little Stephano Company and the Directors proposed that another schooner be acquired. The women shareholders voted unanimously against it. My experience of women in business is that they never object to being paid a dividend; in fact, I believe they would be better pleased with a business that paid 20 per cent. that one that paid 10 per cent., but when it comes to investing money in an enterprise to get that dividend, they never seem to be so anxious. In this case they stood their ground. They were then asked to retire and the male portion of the company decided to obtain another schooner, but would form a new company, A. Kean & Sons.

In time we bitterly regretted that we had not fallen in line with the women. After the meeting we approached our bankers and put up a proposition. We would invest in another schooner for A. Kean & Sons, which would cost $40,000. Our credit was so well established that it was a case of no sooner asked than given. Unfortunately, however, setbacks were in store for us. The so-called "Squires and Coaker" party returned to power, and Coaker sent a message to the mate of the *Prospero,* who had served under me as mate for a long time, to ask him if he would take charge of the *Prospero.* The reply was in the affirmative. On the *Prospero's* arrival at St. John's, Captain W. B. Kean was told that his services were no longer required. This was no surprise to us, for the Government of Newfoundland worked on the principle of "unto the victors belong the spoils."

The *Prospero* for the next four years was a chapter of accidents. Another Government came into power and restored Captain Wes Kean to the command of that ship. He remained in command for several years and became deservedly popular with the people on the coast. When Government decided to build up a trade between St. John's and Halifax, he was chosen as the man to command the *S.S. Portia,* and he is still in command, building up a splendid business of freight and passengers.

In 1921, when the Bowrings appointed W. B. Kean master of the *S.S. Ranger* at the seal fishery, Coaker, who was a passenger from England to the city, sent a message to the Board of Trade asking why they let Bowring's appoint Wes Kean master of one of their ships. But to teach him the object lesson that "it's hard to keep a good man down," Captain W. B. Kean, however, advanced from the *Ranger* to the *Terra Nova* and then to the *Eagle,* and when they decided to send the Red Cross Line steamer *S.S. Sylvia,* the largest ship that ever went to the seal fishery, Captain W. B. Kean was placed in command.

Eventually I went to Nova Scotia and bought a new schooner called the *Little Princess.* We met with reasonable success so far as the running of her was concerned, and in short time we would have got back the money we spent for her and she would be a paying investment. To save paying a high rate of insurance, however, we insured in a French firm. When she was lost we found, to our sorrow, that it was a bankrupt firm and we lost $18,000.

Before finishing my comment on the duel between Coaker and myself, I should like to say that I have aimed at a completely impersonal statement. It is for this reason that these facts find a place in my life's history, and not because I bear any malice. Sir William Coaker and I have met and shaken hands over this matter and nothing has happened since which might lead me to believe that Sir William Coaker would not do me a service if it lay in his power. This will be read by surprise by many of my friends, and will, perhaps, remind them of the words of the distinguished Justice Emerson, "Politics makes strange bedfellows."

It will be remembered how bitterly opposed Squires and Coaker were to each other prior to 1919, and what a surprise their friends had when they heard that these two men had formed an alliance. Such, however, was the case. Squires was chosen as leader and Coaker as leader of the Fishermen's Union—first-lieutenant. They joined forces and went against a party led by Sir Michael Cashin and came back with a sweeping majority. Under that Government the most unprecedented things ever heard of in the history of Responsible Government in this country were done; of these the celebrated Coaker's Fish Regulations formed a part.

In the spring of 1923, a year before another General Election was due,[2] the whole country was startled one morning to hear that almost the whole of the Squires Cabinet had resigned and that Coaker was among them. "Squires has been wounded in the house of his friends" was the cry that was raised by some of Squires' adherents. A truce was made with the Squires-Coaker Government by Mr. Warren, a distinguished lawyer; Coaker and some of the other members of the Squires Cabinet were reinstated, and the so-called Government of Squires and Coaker under Warren as Prime Minister came into power. Warren had pledged himself to his party and the Legislature that a Royal Commission of Inquiry would be held to inquire into the causes which led up to these somewhat strange proceedings, and Warren, true to his promise, went to England. In due course Sir Thomas Hollis Walker came out and conducted an inquiry.

Public scandals in connection with pit-props[3] and other public matters were the outcome of that inquiry, so that when the time came to go to the country in 1924, Warren, seeing that there was no hope of his party being returned, at the eleventh hour threw up the sponge. He thereupon advised the Governor to call on Mr. Coaker to form a party. Coaker declined, and recommended Mr. A. E. Hickman, a merchant and politician who had led the Opposition in the Legislature for some time. Hickman accepted the offer. I was asked to become a member of his party and accepted. This had the effect of bringing me into contact with Coaker. We met in the home of Mr. Hickman in Military Road. After some conversation I pointed out to him where he had been deceived by certain lying rumours which, in the early days of the Union, had been brought to him about me. He assured me that he had seen his mistake.

My mission to Mr. Hickman's house was due to the fact that when I sailed for the seal fishery that year three of my men were drowned by falling through the ice near the entrance of the harbour. I was slated for Bay de Verde, and Hickman was told by my political opponents that because of that accident I would stand no chance of being elected. Mr. Hickman, not wishing to take chances, invited Sir William Lloyd, Coaker and myself for a discussion. For some time Mr. Hickman and Sir William Lloyd were in one room, Mr. Coaker and myself in another. I briefly sketched the cause of our quarrel in the early days of the Union and then related the origin of the accident. When Sir William Lloyd met us, Mr. Coaker said, "Captain Kean has told me all about the accident. I cannot see that there is any blame to be laid on him whatever." So it was arranged that we should meet at a party meeting at Sir William Lloyd's office that afternoon; we met and it was agreed that I should go to Bay de Verde with Mr. Cave as my colleague. When that meeting ended I made towards Mr. Coaker

CAPTAIN JOSEPH W. KEAN'S FUNERAL PROCESSION, WATER STREET WEST. CAPTAIN KEAN WAS LOST ON THE *S.S. FLORIZEL*, 1918. PHOTO: COURTESY MADELINE (KEAN) GOSSE.

THE LARGEST FUNERAL HELD IN ST. JOHN'S. HUNDREDS, PERHAPS THOUSANDS OF SEALERS, IN ST. JOHN'S TO GO TO THE ICE, FOLLOW THE CASKET OF CAPTAIN JOSEPH W. KEAN TO THE GRAVEYARD, 1918. PHOTO: COURTESY OF MADELINE (KEAN) GOSSE.

CAPTAIN JOSEPH W. KEAN'S HORSE-DRAWN CASKET, ST. JOHN'S, 1918. PHOTO: COURTESY MADELINE (KEAN) GOSSE.

ST. JOHN'S, March 1st, 1918.

DEAR

Please accept the sincere thanks of my wife, family, and self; also the wife and family of dear Captain Joe, for your words of sympathy. We believe never was sympathy more sincere, certainly not more universal. The community will miss his genial smile and his very valuable service. We have lost a dutiful son; his wife a devoted husband, and his children the kindest of fathers; his vacant chair can never be filled in his home. His loss to our family is irreparable; time can only heal the wound, and I am afraid some of us will not live long enough for that. Our only comfort is he died without leaving one regret, leaving thousands of friends behind, but not one enemy.

From his grief-stricken Father—

A. KEAN.

CAPTAIN ABRAM'S NOTE OF THANKS TO PERSONS EXPESSING CONDOLENCES ON THE DEATH OF HIS SON, CAPTAIN JOSEPH W. KEAN. PHOTO: COURTESY MADELINE (KEAN) GOSSE.

and said, "Now, let bygones be bygones." Suiting the action to the word, he came towards me and shook hands, and I have good reason to believe he meant it.

You can imagine my surprise next day when I learned that another was taken in my place. I never received a satisfactory explanation from either Mr. Hickman or Cave. I do not lay the blame on Coaker; he and I have since been on speaking terms. Some time after that he sent me a letter asking me where he could get a vessel for Brazil. I chartered my own vessel, the *Cecil Jr.,* and got good satisfaction from him. So ended the controversy between Coaker and myself, and with me there is no malice or ill-will against him. Sir William Coaker is possessed of more than ordinary sense; he had great executive ability, is a great worker, and has undoubtedly been a friend to a great many people.

No sooner had the party, led by Mr. Hickman, been formed than a meeting was called by the opposite party, which Mr. Walter Monroe was chosen to lead. He was a young and ambitious merchant, well known and of good report, and sprung from a good stock. The very name of Monroe must have struck terror in the minds of the other party, for it could plainly be seen from the reports which came from all quarters that was received with acclamation throughout the country.

In 1924 the poll was declared, and Monroe and his party were victorious. They had gone to the country on the policy of "clean up and keep clean," and in my opinion, as far as Monroe was concerned, he meant it and did it. I am convinced that we never had a more honest man at the head of affairs than Monroe since we had Responsible Government, not excepting Sir Robert Bond. Not all his party, however, upheld the motto of cleaning up and keeping clean. Some kicked over the traces, crossed the floor and formed a factious opposition, but it can be said to the credit of the remainder of his party that they held together and saw the end of the term. Monroe, by that time sickened by the treatment he had received from his own party, refused to lead another, but recommended the Hon. F. C. Alderdice, member of the Upper House, to take his place. Brave man that he was, he accepted the position and held office until a General Election in 1928, when a cry was raised to give Squires a second trial. Sir R. A. Squires and Sir William Coaker united their forces again and defeated the Alderdice party. Alderdice himself, however, was elected, and with a few others put up a most formidable opposition.

I took a great interest in temperance. Confederation, annexation with the United States (which was one of Sir Robert Bond's pet theories),[4] Coaker's Fish Regulations and many other public questions received my very best consideration. In fact, in my opinion, we are suffering more in this country today for want of public-spirited men than from any other cause. Goethe says that the public wishes itself to be managed like a woman; one must say nothing to it except what it likes to hear. Steele has said that "Zeal for the public good is the characteristic of a man of honour and a gentleman and must take the place of pleasures, profits, and all other private gratifications."[*]

[1] Cf. J. Hawes: "Every man who loves his country, or wishes well to the best interest of society, will show himself a decided friend, not only of morality and the laws, but of religious institutions, and honourably bear his part in supporting them."

1 The Liberal Party led by Richard Squires and allied with the Union Party under William Coaker won the election.

2 Kean is confused on this point. The scandal broke after Squires had led his party to a second electoral victory in the Spring of 1923.

3 Prior to the 1923 election members of Squires' party had changed bills to the government's pit-prop account.

4 Bond was interested in free trade with the United States, not in annexation.

A WHITECOAT, ONE WEEK OLD

OUT FOR A DAY'S KILLING

CHAPTER VII

My wife's death—A big loan—Humble pie—A trip to Genoa and an unpleasant surprise—Government by Commission—A digression—Bowring Brothers—Temperance

In the political history I have brought you to the year 1928. In my private life's history I want to take you back to 1920. Socially and financially, that year had something worse in store for me than anything I had yet experienced. Sickness invaded my home. My partner in life was stricken with paralysis which laid her helpless, and ended in death, but not until she had lingered with us in that condition for seven years and seven months. So ended the life of an ideal wife, mother and Christian woman.

This same year, 1920, was the year that the administration of the Coaker Fish Regulations had reached its height. Italy had appointed a committee, called the "Consortium," whose duty it was to look after the interests of their fellow countrymen, particularly in food prices. Coaker, on the other hand, wanted to get the highest prices possible for our fish. Ragnolie was head of the Consortium in Italy; Coaker was the head of the Fish Regulation Association in Newfoundland. If he could only get a high price for our fish he would be the white-headed boy.

He was not only head of the Fish Regulation Association, he was also head of the Fishermen's Protective Union, besides being a member of the Executive Government and Minister of Marine and Fisheries. He said, "We will bring the Consortium to their knees." How was that to be brought about? To Coaker it was

51

easy. He issued a proclamation that no one should sell any fish until the price met with his approval. In consequence, scores of our schooners, fish-laden, were laid up in foreign markets waiting for our fish to rise until demurrage[1] swelled out of all proportion.

Anyone of ordinary intelligence or common sense could have seen the folly of such a course. One day I went into the Bank of Nova Scotia and met a man who said to me, "I am surprised at a man of your ability speaking against the Fish Regulation. Why don't you buy a load of fish and send it across yourself?" I said I would if I had the money. He said, "I will lend you the money." I went down to the Board of Trade and told Sir Michael Cashin what had happened. Sir Michael said, "Why didn't you accept his offer?" I said, "I think I will call his bluff." I was the owner of three foreign-going vessels, one of which was at Lisbon, with her demurrage already at about $7,000. Suiting the action to the word I went to the man's office and I said, "I have the *Little Princess* here now ready for a freight and I can't get one. If you will let me have the money I will buy a load of fish and send her across." He replied, "I will go halves with you." I said, "How much money will it require?" He said, "For insurance and all, about $54,000."

I put the matter to my bankers. They agreed, and I went back and closed the bargain, never doubting his ability to pay. I commenced loading the schooner and drew cheques on my own bank up to the sum of $27,000, and then drew on my associate at the Bank of Nova Scotia until I got $20,000, whereupon the manager informed me I could get no more. I went to my partner to find he was a sick man in bed. There were 1,300 quintals to pay for and an export tax of $1,200 to pay or there would be trouble. At last the manager of the Bank of Nova Scotia said, "Captain, I will let you have all you want in your own name." There was nothing for me to do but accept the offer, which I did. The schooner then finished loading and sailed for the foreign market. In due course she arrived at a port in Spain and waited until we were advised by the head of our Fish Regulations what price we should sell for. In the meantime demurrage had risen out of all proportion to anything we had known before. The owners of cargoes realized every day that the fish became of less value and then a demand was made to Coaker to lift the Regulations.

The *Little Princess* went to Genoa and sold the cargo to Ragnolie, the chairman of the Consortium. Before he commenced discharging, my captain said, "I want to wire my owners how much you intend giving us per quintal for our cargo of fish." He replied, "You may wire your owners that I will put your fish in cold storage when it is landed. I will pay your freight when I can. I will sell it to the best advantage, and you may inform your owners if they are not satisfied with that you may take your fish elsewhere."

That fish was shipped in Genoa in the early part of January. I never got round until late in August, when I went to the Board of Trade one day and met the late Hon. R. K. Bishop, who had shipped a cargo at the same time. He told me that he had heard that things were looking up in the fish markets, and I made up my mind to go to Genoa and see what could be done. I interviewed my associate and he promised to pay half the expenses. I saw the managers of the two banks, who thought I was well advised. Early in September I sailed from New York in a 12,000 ton ship, the *S.S. Ryndom*. The trip across to England will ever be remembered among the pleasant memories of the past. I was landed, with three or four other passengers, in a tender on the south coast of England, while the *Ryndom* sailed for France and other ports towards her destination.

Late in the afternoon I arrived in London. Next day I went to Holmwood & Holmwood, who were our London agents, and explained my mission. They very kindly gave me an interpreter and we embarked for Genoa. After arriving at Genoa, we went to Mr. Ragnolie, and I am free to confess he was the first man I ever met who did not seem to take me at face value. After my interpreter had explained the purport of our mission he replied, "I am very sorry but I do not know Captain Kean." I asked him if he did not know I was the owner of the *Little Princess.* He replied, "The man who got the documents from the Royal Bank of Canada in London is the only man from whom I had to take my instructions, and that man was Mr. William Munn." He advised me when the cargo was sold to pay over the proceeds to the credit of my associate in the Bank of Nova Scotia in London. When my interpreter told him my side of the story he promised to stay proceedings until he had heard from me after I got back to Newfoundland.

Next day I passed through Rome on my way to Naples and saw some historic sight at Naples. At Naples I saw the ruins of Pompeii and visited Governor Harris' daughter, who was living at Naples. The next day I went back to London. On my arrival there I asked Holmwood & Holmwood for some explanation of the extraordinary proceedings. After some investigation they found that my letter of instructions when the cargo was shipped had been overlooked. For this they expressed extreme regret. Then they went with me to the Royal Bank of Canada and asked the bank to instruct Mr. Ragnolie to pass over to the Royal Bank of Canada the proceeds of the *Little Princess* cargo, and not to pay out any part of it until they had heard from me from Newfoundland.

When I arrived at St. John's I went to my associate's office to find that he was sick in bed. I made out a message for him to send to Ragnolie (without even consulting him as to what it was about). The message read: "Please pay over to my account in the Royal Bank of Canada in London all the proceeds of the *Little Princess* cargo." In this I had the concurrence of Mr. William Munn; I then asked them both to sign it and they did so without demur. I had good reason to believe that Ragnolie and our Prime Minister at that time, Sir R. A. Squires, were very great friends. I thereupon went to Sir Richard and asked him to forward a message to Mr. Ragnolie as to my identity, offering to pay for the message, but he very kindly consented to do so without charge, and in less than forty-eight hours Sir Richard received a reply from Ragnolie: "Inform Captain Kean proceeds of *Little Princess* cargo paid over to the Royal Bank of Canada in London." In due course I was furnished with a full account, among other items being a bill for cold storage of $12,000. The cargo had been insured for every sort of claim until the total reached $83,000. With the amount for cold storage and insurance, my loss was about $10,000. I paid my associate his part, thinking the amount I had on his account at the Bank of Nova Scotia would be settled. To my surprise, however, not one dollar was paid, and I was held completely responsible. This I entirely disputed. After some years debating the matter, Mr. Young, the manager, gentleman that he was, compromised with me and I accepted and paid.

One night in 1927 the Prime Minister, Mr. Monroe, called me over the phone and asked me if I would accept a position as member of the Legislative Council, or what is called in England the House of Lords, and in America the Senate. I accepted and thanked him, for neither Mr. Monroe nor any member of his party owed me anything. The very fact that I had not asked for it convinced me that the Prime Minister believed that, owing to my long experience in public life and the great interest I had taken in public matters, I would be a fit and proper person to fill that position. Whether he was right in his conjecture or not the public is the best judge. I brought the account of the political history of the country down to 1928, with Squires and Coaker in power. After the poll was declared a procession with music and cheering started from the cross-roads in the west end until a hall was reached in the centre of the town, and speeches were made in which they spent some time patting one another on the back, but on the whole I heard no one complain.

Things proceeded in much the same way. When money could not be found to balance the budget, it was borrowed by the million for that purpose and for other expenditure. 1929 and 1930 were uneventful, but in 1932 it was found that our credit was stopped in the money markets of the world. A General Election followed. The Hon. F. C. Alderdice led a party against the Government and came back with an overwhelming majority. He succeeded in having a Royal Commission of Inquiry set up to look into our affairs. This Commission recommended that for some years at least we should abandon our form of Representative Government and be ruled by a Commission. One thing that can be said to the credit of Mr. Alderdice is that he so managed matters that he instilled sufficient courage into his party to vote themselves out of power three years before the time fixed for a General Election.

I had been born in the year that we first secured Responsible Government, and I was in the Legislative Council and voted for the Commission. It is only fair to say, however, that I only took the latter course because I saw no other alternative. I still believe in our right to govern ourselves, and I believe we have men in the country well equipped for the task. That we were brought to our present position is not due to our form of government, but because the people made the wrong choice. We have many men fit to rule us, but they could not stand the persecution, which is inevitable, to secure the position.

In my opinion we have lost the right to rule ourselves not because we did not possess enough intelligence, but because we lacked moral courage to dare to do the right. We permitted irresponsible and immoral men to fill positions of eminence of trust, for which neither nature nor grace ever intended them. Moreover, too many of us kept silent when we should have been outspoken. Our form of government was a facsimile of that of Great Britain. The difference between us today is that Great Britain raised the standard and taught the people that they should measure up to it. Unfortunately for His Majesty's oldest colony, we lowered the standard and fell and lost that which we should have had today. We now occupy the humiliating position of not having the right to govern ourselves. The old adage has proved true in our case—we have sown to the wind and we are now reaping the whirlwind.[2]

If there is one aspect of my life's history which has been more significant than any other it is the seal fishery, and I could not do justice to that without introducing the name of the old-established firm of Bowring Brothers. Of forty-five years spent in commanding ships at the seal fishery, thirty-three years were given up to commanding ships from that firm. I not only wish to stress the number of ships commanded from that firm, but the class of ships that I had.

This question is indeed the central point of my narrative, for on it turns the nature of my achievement in having brought a million seals to port. The fact may be overlooked by many that no man could have lived long enough to accomplish what I have in small-sized ships, but in the service of Bowring Brothers I was given charge of the *S.S. Florizel*, the *S.S. Stephano*, also the *Nascopie*, and last, but by no means least, the *S.S. Beothic*. These ships ranged from 1,700 tons to 3,400 tons gross, and I was offered the command of each of the above-named ships by the head of the firm, without my applying for them. I may add in passing that I was offered the command of the *Imogene* before she was built (for I think I was the first to see her blue-print outside the members of the firm), but owing to my having been appointed master of the *Nascopie* I did not think it right to break my agreement. Had I done so, I should long since have brought in my millionth seal.

I have read and studied the lives of great men, and I found without exception, that great men distinguished themselves, not so much by the success they achieved, as by their ability to grapple with difficulties and overcome them. I was three times shipwrecked. Once when I lost my fishing schooner in 1885, which I referred to in another place in my history. I left home full of hope for a successful summer, and in less than forty-eight hours all my hopes were dashed to the ground. In 1896 I lost the *S.S. Wolf* twenty-seven hours after leaving home. My loss was far greater than most men know. The anticipated loss of a load of seals for that year was in itself bad enough, for I think it will not be disputed that when I lost my ship we were nearer to the seals than any other ship in the fleet, as subsequent events proved, for the two most successful ships for that season passed through our wreckage before reaching the seals. This same year I had supplied the outfits for my crew and never had one dollar's insurance, and when the *Wolf* sank out of sight there went with her two thousand dollars of my hard earnings.

From the day I took charge of ships until the present time I have had under my command considerably over one hundred thousand people.[3] The only accident was in 1924, when three of my crew fell through a treacherous slob pan of ice and were drowned less than half a mile from the harbour of St. John's. Once, while master of the mail boat, a lunatic jumped over the stern of the ship and we lowered the boat and rescued him, and by applying first aid, brought him to life again. Another time, when entering the harbour of St. John's, another man jumped overboard. As there was no chance of stopping the ship without running the risk of putting the ship on shore, I noticed two motor-boats coming out. I caught the megaphone and informed them of what had happened, and before I docked I had the satisfaction of knowing that the one of the motor-boats had saved the man, none the worse except for a good ducking, which may have done him more good than harm.

It will be noted that I have occupied different positions. At the age of thirteen I began cod fishing and worked at that industry for twenty years, ten of which I was master. For fourteen years I was in the mercantile business. Eight years I served as representative of the people in the House of Assembly; for some of this time I was a member of the Executive, and I was the first acting Minister of Marine and Fisheries. Altogether I was nineteen years in charge of the Coastal Service, three years on Labrador, and sixteen years on the Northern Service of Newfoundland. I have been a member of the Legislative Council since 1927. When I say I was forty-seven years a master at the seal fishery, it must be recalled that the seal fishery only lasts two months in each year, and I occupied the positions mentioned above during the same years I went to the seal fishery.

Like most of my fellow men I have left undone the things I ought to have done, and done some things that I ought not to have done. I have always been a great temperance advocate—I am still, but I take no credit for being temperate. I could not be otherwise, for I hate drunkenness as I hate poison. I am strongly in favour of temperance on account of the innocent victims, hundreds of thousands of women and children today who are suffering through no fault of their own. Instead of being supported and fitted for positions in life by those they are depending on, the money that should have gone for this support has been worst than wasted, and these dependents have been doomed to be hewers of wood and drawers of water. Worse still, in these years of depression they cannot get the wood to hew or even water to draw. I have said that I took no credit for being temperate as I could not be otherwise. In fact, as far as I am aware, none of the Kean family has ever been an habitual drunkard.

The besetting sin of the Kean family seems to have been profanity. Being of a hasty temper myself, when quite a young man I had a strong inclination to indulge in that filthy habit. How well I conquered that habit others can testify, for out of over one hundred thousand people that I commanded, I challenge one of them to say I ever called him other than his name. In fact, I made it a point to rebuke my officers at the Coastal Service and at the seal fishery for swearing, and I have been often complimented by passengers on the absence of any profane language on the ships that I have commanded at the Coastal Service. Often my men at the seal fishery have asked my pardon when they have forgotten themselves and used profane language in my presence. Unfortunately many of our otherwise good public men ruin themselves by indulging in this vice. Indeed, the man is to be pitied who cannot find enough words in the English language without descending to such vile substitutes.

1 Demurrage is the charge for detaining a vessel beyond the time agreed upon in the original contract.

2 This explanation for Newfoundland's loss of Responsible Government was fairly widespread in Kean's time. However, today most agree that the collapse of international trade because of the Great Depression created a situation that Newfoundland could not cope with on its own.

3 Over one hundred thousand man-seasons (as in man-years).

THE S.S. FLORIZEL, DOWN IN THE WATER, ON THE ROCKS AT CAPPAHAYDEN. ON BOARD WAS ABRAM KEAN'S SON, PASSENGER CAPTAIN JOSEPH KEAN, WHO DID NOT SURVIVE. (PHOTO: CENTRE FOR NEWFOUNDLAND STUDIES ARCHIVES)

CHAPTER VIII

*Fish curing—-The Bay Bulls plant and its critics—Flakes—Sir
Wilfred Grenfell and St. Anthony—The Grenfell Mission—
Labrador—An Eskimo on trial*

I commenced writing the history of my life in St. John's, and
some of it I wrote in Battle Harbour. Today I am at Alexis
River, Labrador, on board the *Miss Newfoundland*, owned by Mr.
Gerald S. Doyle, who kindly asked me to accompany him here
from Battle Harbour. I do not know for what reason, for if no one
bought more of his patent medicine than I have, he would never
have amassed his fortune. However, it is a pleasure to gain his
favour for he is jolly and generous, even to a fault, and it is
questionable if ever Dr. Chase had a better advertiser of his wares
than Mr. G. S. Doyle.

I have mentioned the many positions I have occupied during
my lifetime, pointing out that I commenced life at the age of
thirteen at the cod fishery. The casual reader may think that, like
most men, I merely served my time catching fish, that as master,
like a great many masters, I did my best to get all I could and tried
to get the best price possible for the proceeds of the voyage,
paying little or no attention to quality. Such was not the case. My
father, in his day, was noted for his ability to prepare cod seines[1]
for hauling fish, and during his life had scores of seines brought
to him to be prepared for that work. I served my time with my
father in the net loft until I became as proficient as he was in the
work. My father built his own boats and his own stores. I did the

61

same; consequently when I was master at the fishery I prepared my own seine, I prepared my own traps, I built my own boats and I built my own stores. I have been master salter of the voyage as well as master splitter. During the time I was master, if, through circumstances over which I had no control, I had some bad fish, I lost more perspiration over it that I did over any other thing. In this year of grace 1934, under the Commission Government, I have been appointed Fisheries Officer on the coast of Labrador.

I must emphasize at this point that all the fish I saw last year and this year in salt bulk was, in my opinion, perfect. There is no doubt in my mind that the fish becomes bad in the process of making. Various reasons may be given for this. For instance, making fish in hot sun with calm weather will be likely to give sunburnt fish. Water-horse fish[2] spread on the rocks with no covering and in bad weather is doomed to become inferior fish, and it is lamentable how this generation has fallen from the practice of their fathers in that respect. Our fathers of fifty years ago would no more think of going to the fishery before they first of all provided rinds for covering their fish than they would think of going without first getting salt with which to cure.

An enormous amount of literature is distributed today to teach our people how to make fish. This, some people think, is the development of science, which at its best is only getting back to first principles or doing as our fathers did before us. Last year I reported seeing fish spread on the bawn,[3] and traces of all sorts of animals could be seen among the fish. Right here on the Labrador, fish and dogs are so close together that I see no reason why the dogs should go hungry. Every report I have made on this point has been pigeon-holed, and I have been told by those in authority that we cannot afford to publish things of that nature. My own reason for writing on this point in connection with my life's history is because owing to the position I now hold I am brought face to face with it. If you wish to bring about reform in the curing of fish, you must see that all dogs are pounded in during fish-making (even Eskimos, I am told, separate the dogs from the fish); insist that every fisherman has covering for his fish to shelter it from fresh water; no talqual[4] is good, a strict cull is better, but both combined is no good if number one is mixed with number two for the foreign markets. The above remarks may, and I have no doubt will, bring upon me a certain amount of ridicule. My only apology is the great desire I have to bring back this great industry to its former standing and bring back prosperity again to our people.

Reform is not an easy task. A great many people have tried to bring it about and failed. The few that have succeeded are like angels' visits, few and far between.

The right of free speech seems a very simple thing, yet it has come to us comparatively quite recently, and only through rivers of blood. The attempt to bring about scientific reform in connection with our fisheries will take a long time and it will cost a lot of money; a remedy will never be found until the disease is first of all located. That disease will not be found in reform schools or in first-class colleges. One would have a much better chance of finding it in the fishing stages of our people today, especially if one can compare the fishing stage of fifty years ago with the fishing stage of today.

When it comes to the stores for putting up dried fish, in many cases there is no comparison because there is no store there. Recently I listened to one of our leading fishermen giving a lecture concerning the great good that has come to us by scientific investigation of our fisheries. He spoke in glowing terms of the Bay Bulls[5] plant, and no doubt from his point of view, he could give very good reasons. If I were called upon to give my opinion of the ability of the men in charge and their scientific knowledge, I would first of all have to admit that I know nothing whatever about the business and therefore considered my opinion worthless. But if I were called up to say what has to been done to improve the cure of our fish, I should say without fear of successful contradiction that we have sent more bad fish out of this country since the Bay Bulls plant has been in existence than ever before in my recollection of the same period. It would certainly be the height of folly to blame the Bay Bulls plant for that. It is equally ridiculous to say that the Bay Bulls plant has offered us any remedy.

Before leaving this important subject I must refer to bait depots. Last winter in the M.C.L.I. [Methodist College Literary Institute] we debated this question; the affirmative was led by one of our most able lawyers, the negative by myself. The negative convinced the majority that bait depots were an expensive business that we could not afford, in other words, that it never would be a paying proposition. In the course of my remarks I pointed out that it was bad to have plenty of fish but no bait, but that very often a much worse state of things prevailed, namely, plenty of bait but no fish.

In referring to Green Bay and White Bay I pointed out that the scarcity of fish in these two bays last year was not due to a scarcity of bait but of fish. In these two bays this year there is an abundance of fish and plenty of bait, which renders your bait depots useless, although they cost hundreds of dollars which must be paid for by the taxpayers of this country or of England. In saying this I am prepared to admit that the Commission has acted to the best of its ability, with an eye to the welfare of this country, but for some time yet it will have to grope its way in the dark and, through no fault of its own, in some matters will probably be poorly advised.

The next topic I wish to discuss is flakes for the making of fish. In a former chapter in speaking of rinds I should have mentioned the getting of boughs for flakes. In my early days I was never taught to spread water-horse fish on lungars[6] or rocks until it had first been spread on flakes for two or three days, as it had a tendency to make the fish sodden. The advantage of flakes is that the pure air gets on the back and face together. There has been no attempt on the part of anyone to explain how it is that our fish is not as good as it used to be. Only the elder people know the difference, but many of them are too indifferent to inquire into its causes. It is sometimes acknowledged that we became careless during the war.[7] Moreover, a great many of those with enough interest to write on the matter seem to have but one string to their bow, that is, that we have lost the art of making good fish, and we must trust to science to provide a remedy.

I am a great believer in science, but I have never yet come to the conclusion that I should expect science to do for me what I ought to do for myself. William Mathews says: "A great deal of the joy of life consists in doing perfectly, or at least to the best of one's ability, everything which he attempts to do. There is a sense of satisfaction, a pride in surveying such a work, a work which is rounded, full, exact, complete in all its parts—which the superficial man, who leaves his work in a sloven, slipshod, half-finished condition, can never know. It is this conscientious completedness which turns work into art. The smallest work well done becomes artistic."

In writing the history of an active life of service in this world, if one is not careful one may dwell too much on the vicissitudes of life or, in other words, like flies that stick to the sores of the horse's back, we may stick to the faults and not take the blessings. To avoid that I want to make it perfectly clear that I am not one of those who believes that this world is a vale of tears or, as some put it, that it is a howling wilderness; in fact, when I hear people talk that way I believe they are the dogs that are doing the howling. I am prepared to believe with the Rev. S. Small that this is just such a world as a kind father would give to his children for three score years and ten, and yet it is remarkable how many of us there are that lose faith in God and humanity.

Only the other day I was introduced to a man who in many respects seemed a very intelligent man, but before we were talking very long he expressed the belief that the whole cause of our trouble is that we are all dishonest. When I pointed out to him that I thought that this was a rather sweeping statement to make, and that I thought if I told him he was a dishonest man he would not like it, he unhesitatingly said he meant himself. I told him he had a perfect right to speak for himself, but that he had no right to speak for me. A little later in the conversation he said that one cause of our trouble was that men of means did not give their money to their poorer neighbours. An hour or so later when I spoke to his boss who introduced him to me, I said, "That skipper of yours seems to be a great talker." He replied, "Did you draw him out on stocks and shares? That man has made some fine investments; he is worth a lot of money." And yet I could not gather from anything he said to me that he was worth any money or that he had ever given away one dollar to his next-door neighbour. All that he tried to impress upon me was that if I ever met an honest man he would have hairs on the palms of his hands.

I do not believe any such nonsense, and if I ever do meet a man with hairs on the palms of his hands, I will not attribute it to his honesty, but rather to the fact that he is a good-for-nothing, lazy vagabond, who, if he had worked for a living as he should have done, would have no hairs there. The men and women who put these foolish obstructions in the way of well-meaning people who are doing the best they can towards bringing about reform do no good but, on the contrary, retard progress and hinder rather than help reform.

A thousand times more good can be found in that poem written by an American poetess, many years ago, namely:

"Don't look for the flaws as you go through life,
And even if you find them it is wise to be mind
And be somewhat blind and look for the good
     behind them.
For the cloudiest night has a tinge of light
Somewhere in its shadows hiding.
It is better by far to hunt for a star,
Than the spots of the sun to abide in.
The world can never adjust itself

To suit all your whims to the letter.
Something will go wrong, your whole lives long,
And the sooner you know it the better.
It is folly to fight with the infinite,
And go under at last in the wrestle,
But wise is the man who shapes unto God's plan,
As the water shapes into the vessel."

The one man who has profited by the above advice is Dr. Grenfell, perhaps better known as Sir Wilfred Grenfell, a man who may be prepared to admit that he has made some mistakes, who perhaps has altered his tactics many times, but whose life has been one of activity. No man can speak with better authority of the life-work of that man than I can. All his life's work on the Labrador and Newfoundland has been performed in my time. I first knew of him when he laboured among our fishermen on the Labrador coast. The fact that I was master of the Northern mail boat brought me in contact with his marvellous development in St. Anthony. I have carried hundreds of patients there before there was a wharf for them to land from at the Grenfell Mission, and I know something of the opposition that had to be met by the powers that be, before they got the right of way to get one there.

Those who saw St. Anthony before the Grenfell Mission and have seen it today can speak with some authority on the great success that has attended the efforts of Sir Wilfred Grenfell. Sir Wilfred is a man of many parts. His first work was to instil the right spirit among the people, and he was broad-minded enough not to aim at any one denomination. If you put the question to Dr. Grenfell, "Am I my brother's keeper?" quick as lightning you would get the reply, in no uncertain manner, "Yes!" Never in all my experience have I found men more ready to help or co-operate with one another regardless of creed than I did from Englee to Griquet. He taught the people to apply first aid, and I have no hesitation in saying that you will not find a greater number of people anywhere on our coast more proficient in that work than in St. Anthony and its vicinity. He laboured in the cause of education. The customs officer is from St. Anthony; the magistrate is a resident of Griquet. He educated a resident of Labrador and he became the architect of the St. Anthony Hospital. Many of the homes of the people have running water, some have electric light. Gardening has improved one hundred per cent. A floating dock has been built by the side of the wharf of the Grenfell Mission, and this is perhaps of more practical benefit than any other of its kind in Newfoundland. Such achievements show what can be done by the efforts of one man who starts out with a single eye to do good, and a determination to meet difficulties and overcome them. How they have been met and conquered no one can tell better than Sir Wilfred himself.

Before leaving this subject, I think it is only fair to say that Sir Wilfred Grenfell would have found it hard to have met a better class of people for his work than at St. Anthony, for the Moore family, who were doing a mercantile business there for many years, had established the best feeling between supplier and supplied that it ever was my pleasure to find. In that respect I think Sir Wilfred was fortunate.

On the question of making good fish I have said, "Fish and dogs are so mixed up that I see no reason why the dogs should go hungry." In fact I have been so much puzzled over the number of dogs roving around and no one complaining, that I felt it was a very difficult matter to approach, as everyone needs dogs for his winter's work and they had all agreed to disagree on the matter. I did not have to wait long, however.

Silas Gardener from Trinity Bay and Robert Holloway from Bonavista Bay, both of them stationed here for summer fishing, called to ask me if there was no law against dogs roving at large during fish-making, and complained that they were a source of continual annoyance and were continually tearing and destroying their fish. One man, Robert Holloway, said they had torn up ten fish out of a small lot he had spread the day before, and that one of his neighbours told him he estimated that the dogs last year destroyed ten quintals of fish belonging to him. Later on in the afternoon when I went on Baine Johnston's wharf I found another man complaining to Mr. S. Loveridge, the Agent for Baine Johnston, about the same thing. He said that one night last year the dogs got at one of the piles of fish on his flake and spoiled three quintals. Mr. Silas Gardener told me the other morning that they found one of the dogs in one of their blubber puncheons; fortunately, he said, it was fresh liver, but they got it out.

Both Gardener and Holloway told me that men, women and children drank out of the same wells; there was nothing to prevent the dogs from drinking out of the same well as the human beings. This report came from Westward Island. Before this I was inquiring where the water came from that I was drinking, and I was told it came from a spring and was protected by a concrete basement. I thought I would go and make a survey of the two wells on this side. Just as I had been told, I found a concrete basement over the well, but the good lady of the house where I am staying complained that the cover had gone again and said that the cover had been destroyed several times; their neighbours used to cut them up for firewood. Much to my surprise, I found the well but a few feet away from an old cemetery. The cemetery was so much higher than the well that there is no doubt whatever that those who drank would have the full benefit of the drainings of those who went before them.

I am no authority as to how the great Creator provided that the filtering of water through the earth purifies it for human consumption, but I am fully persuaded that if it were not for that wise provision, many of us would not be alive today to tell the tale. The well on the western side of the island also had a concrete wall and a cover but neither of the wells had a fence around them to protect them from dogs or other animals. Yesterday I sent the following message to the Department of Natural Resources:

"Mr. P. FUDGE, Chief Fishery Officer.

Silas Gardener of Trinity Bay and Robert Holloway of Bonavista at Battle Harbour complain of dogs being at large while fish is making. Holloway says he had ten fish torn to pieces today. Is there any redress. Please reply.
     A. KEAN, Labrador fishery officer.

Twenty-four hours passed but there was no reply. It was reported that Sir John Hope Simpson and others of the Commission were coming to Labrador, and it may be that they will take action themselves, which would be the proper thing to do.

Recently I visited St. Mary's River in Lewis Bay, the home of the Grenfell Mission. It has a beautiful land-locked harbour which is unfortunately rather shallow. It has a mud bottom and a dredge would probably improve it considerably. The doctor in charge seems very much interested in the work. Already there is a fine hospital and a good-sized school which in the winter months accommodates forty children. They are beginning to take an interest in agriculture and have three or four horned cattle, several pigs and much poultry. This summer they have sown some hay seed with a view to raising for cattle-feeding.

Mr. Samuel Grant with his family, formerly of Trinity, is anchored in the harbour and intends to settle down there and open a commercial business. I was invited on board his yacht with Dr. Moret and his wife. We stayed to dinner and had a very enjoyable time. Judging from the good feeling which exists between Dr. and Mrs. Moret and Mr. and Mrs. Grant, they intend to pull together and make St. Mary's River a truly worthwhile settlement.

Mr. Samuel Grant seems to possess some of that pioneer spirit which made the Western Hemisphere what it is today. Men left crowded cities where there was no outlet for their energy and no room for them to get homes for themselves. As one man put it, they "went into the wilds of the West with nothing but an axe, a gun and a match-box." How far these men succeeded can be gauged by the cities of North-West Canada and by the marvellous development in the Western States of the United States of America.

For many a year one question has constantly been asked: What is the significance of Labrador to the Newfoundlanders? When one remembers how few people from Newfoundland have settled on Labrador from Battle Harbour to Hopedale, there seems some justification for that question. When one considers the continual supply of codfish on Labrador,[8] the new turn which salmon fishery has taken, the new industry of cutting pit-props started in Alexis River, and finally Mr. Grant's new venture, one wonders if history will repeat itself and we shall see from this small beginning the growth of a great industrial movement which will place Labrador on the map as a great industrial centre for the people of Newfoundland. I have no doubt that thousands of my fellow men will pray that such may be the case, for in my experience I have not known so many men walking about with nothing to do and with plenty of time to do it. The sorry part of it is that so many of them seem satisfied with their lot and prepared to take the dole without a murmur, except to complain of the insufficiently of the daily allowance.

The news that has just reached Labrador, that henceforth no one will be allowed to ship fish after sunset or before sunrise, will be received with consternation in some quarters. Many arguments will be advanced for the continuance of the practice, and objections to pure food laws will have to be met and overcome as they have been in other countries. No law made by God or man has ever met with general favour. Only a few days ago on board the *S.S. Kyle* I was ordered, as Justice of the Peace, by the Commission of Justice for Newfoundland to try an Eskimo for breaking into the Hudson Bay Company's Post at Hebron, in Labrador, on two occasions, and stealing goods to the value of $190. As soon as it was rumoured that I would try the case I received some free advice. First, that it was most unfair to try a man who did not know our language; second, that the Hudson Bay Company was possibly to blame because these Eskimos were charged so much for their goods that they committed these offenses in order to bring matters to a head and secure better treatment for the Eskimo for the future.

The man I tried was named Rinatus Tuglavania. He pleaded guilty and admitted that he was the ringleader. I moved very cautiously. Before charging the prisoner, I addressed the Court and dealt with technical objections by quoting the law bearing on the subject from the Statutes of the country. Fortunately for me there was a Moravian missionary on board who could speak the Eskimo language. I asked him to read my judgment to the prisoner. He kindly consented, and before he had finished the prisoner admitted his guilt and pleaded that he would never repeat the offence. I was satisfied that the ends of justice were met. Rinatus Tuglavania had learned his lesson.

After the proceedings were over, I met a young lady who was present and said, "Well, can you speak Eskimo after that?" She said, "But, Captain, who is going to look after that man's wife and family?" I felt she was not speaking for herself for she was too young to voice such an opinion, but she was expressing the opinion of a large number in the Court whose false sympathy had got the better of their judgment. Subsequent events proved that this was the case, for when Sergeant Squibb took the prisoner to Twillingate lockup, he had his pockets full of tobacco, cigarettes and money, given to him, no doubt, by the passengers. Yet this man received justice in accordance with the laws of Great Britain, on whose domain the sun never sets. Mr. Bancroft, in his "History of the United States," says: "The law of Nature is the law of God, irreversible itself and superseding all human law, it perfectly reconciles the true interest and happiness of the universal whole."

The laws and constitution of the English Government are the best in the world because they approach nearest to the laws God has established in our natures. Those who have attempted this barbarous violation of the most sacred rights of their country deserve the name of rebels and traitors, since they not only have violated the laws of their King and country but the laws of Heaven itself.

1 Cod seines were used in shallow water before the invention and widespread acceptance of the cod traps in the 1880s.

2 Fish taken from salt bulk and washed was sometimes referred to as "water-horse fish."

3 Rocky surface on which fish was spread in order to dry. On much of the Labrador coast fish was dried on the bawn out on the island of Newfoundland where wood was plentiful most fish was dried on wooden flakes.

4 The practice of buying fish from fishermen without culling or grading it was referred to as buying "talqual." Buying talqual was blamed for the decline in the quality of Newfoundland's salt fish.

5 A fisheries research facility had been established at Bay Bulls and some thought it a waste of money.

6 Long wooden poles.

7 During the First World War fish prices were extremely high - even for fish of lesser quality.

8 In Newfoundland fisheries terminology "Labrador" was often used to mean "the Labrador coast." Thus to fish on the Labrador was a common expression.

ON THE TRAIL

ON THE TRAIL

CHAPTER IX

*The codfishery laws—Jiggers—The Pouch Cove dispute—Cod
and motor-boats—The Bait Act—Herring-fishery laws—Scottish
practice—Seal-killing*

On my arrival from Labrador I found a letter awaiting me
from a friend who thinks that this work should not be merely
an account of my own life. My reply to that is that if I only
intended to write my personal history I should now be at the end
of my narrative. However, having taken an active part in the
fisheries of this country, I should like to say something about the
laws laid down from time to time to govern that industry.

I will commence with the laws governing the cod fishery. I
was yesterday given a copy of the "Rules and Regulations
Respecting the Fisheries of Newfoundland, 1933." This book
contains 140 pages. After a glance at some of the restrictions I am
convinced that we may dispense with a hundred pages, for I am
fundamentally opposed to a law which prohibits a man from
getting a fish out of the water any way he can, provided that he
gets it honestly and conforms to the law of setting his trap or
other gear away from any trap or other gear previously set. Let
me illustrate by quoting from the "Rules and Regulations." Page
12, Clause 29 states that the use of jiggers is prohibited in the
waters between Round Head and Cape Fogo (both inclusive)
inside the Three Mile Limit from the 1st of July until the 10th of
October in each year. Page 13, Sub-section B of Clause 32
contains the following: "No cod trap shall be set on the fishing

grounds at Tom Cod Rock, Elliott Rock, S.S.W. Rock, George Abbott's Rock and John Abbott's Rock. Cod traps may be set at the southern part of James Island." I could cite fifty more prohibitions of a similar nature, the necessity for which only the people who made them and the Lord Himself know. A final instance will suffice. Page 13, Clause 31 says: "No caplin shall be taken for any other purpose than that of the fisheries during a period of five days after the first arrival anywhere around the caplin grounds of Greenspond, Puffin Island, Copper Island, Newell's Island, Ship Island, Great Island and Wings Island in Bonavista Bay." How long that has been in existence I do not know, but I do know that a similar law was in existence over sixty years ago at Pool's Island, Mr. Job Davis, father of Mr. Joseph Davis, at Valley Field, being appointed to see that the law was enforced.

To deal with jiggers first. From my earliest recollection I have heard people denounce the use of jiggers in connection with the cod fishery, declaring that if the use of jiggers were not stopped, the cod fishery would soon become a thing of the past. Naturally enough, these laws were first put into force in the districts around St. John's, Conception Bay and Trinity Bay, where most of the wise law-makers live. What has been the result? Have St. John's, Conception Bay and Trinity Bay held their own better than the northern bays? Not at all; no one of ordinary intelligence or common sense will contend that the prohibition of jiggers in these southern bays has caused a decline in the fisheries.[1]

It is equally ridiculous to maintain that the prohibition has made any appreciable difference in the catch. Whereas one considers the question of the Labrador, every man seems to be a law unto himself, and jigging has been going on for the last hundred and fifty years, at least, and is still going on today. There has been no time in my life when fish have been so plentiful on Labrador as in the last four years, and whole loads of fish have been jigged. Last Saturday night Captain Frank Thornhill came on board the *Kyle* and told me that his crew had jigged 1,300 quintals. He added, "I have some more salt and I am going off to the White Bears to finish up," remarking that they averaged about 60 quintals per day with the jiggers at Cape Horizon. Captain Arthur Sampson at Cape Horizon told me he had 2,400 quintals and thought trapping was over, but he said, "We can jig all we want." The fact remains that while our law-makers are puzzling their brains about preserving our codfish, the Great Creator made them so cannibalistic they destroy themselves by the million. My attention was drawn to this because the last load of fish I ever killed on Labrador was fed upon its own species. Some of the larger ones had tom cods in their stomachs large enough to split. The same is true of caplin. While we are making laws to protect them, millions of the male caplin every year milk on the spawn until they die, come to the surface and float away by hundreds of millions.

In 1899, when I was acting Minister of Marine and Fisheries, the people of Pouch Cove were much perplexed over the fact that the only way they could get fish was with trawls. For some reason or other fish would not trap, would not net and would not hook. Not all the people had trawls, and these petitioned the Fishery Board to prohibit their use, pointing out that if the use of trawls were permitted the inhabitants would be ruined. The Government said to me, "The best you can do is to take your Deputy and go to Pouch Cove and try and settle this trouble." When we started next morning, Mr. Watson, my Deputy and an older man, said to me, "I believe every settlement should settle their own method of catching fish in the place where they belong." I held exactly the opposite position. We debated the question on the way to Pouch Cove; I don't know if one single argument I used changed Mr. Watson's opinion; I am certain that nothing he said changed mine.

We arrived at Pouch Cove and held an outdoor meeting, hearing the pros and cons from the Pouch Cove people. After hearing all that was said I told them I would present their case to the Fishery Board at St. John's the next day. I assured them that if I succeeded every man in Pouch Cove would have the absolute right to get a fish out of the water any way he chose as long as he got it honestly and conformed to the law as to setting his gear the distance required by law from the gear previously set by his neighbour. The Fishery Board accepted my ruling, which I announced to the people of Pouch Cove the next morning. Late that fall, in October or November, as I was walking up Water Street, a man tapped me on the shoulder. When I turned around he said, "You remember you came down to settle the question about the use of trawls?"[2] I said, "Yes." "Well," he said, "we all had to use trawls; we could not get fish any other way, and we got the best voyage in Pouch Cove we have had for twenty years."

Let me illustrate another point. When the late Joseph Elliott of Change Islands used the first motor-boat for the cod fishery, a number of petitions were got up around Change Islands, Fogo and vicinity, protesting against the practice, pointing out that in shallow water the noise would drive the fish from the ground. However, as soon as the fishermen discovered the benefit of motor-boats their stock went up and the opposition evaporated. In a very short time when the skipper men commenced to ship their crews it was no uncommon question for the sharemen to ask, "Have you got a motor-boat?" and if the answer was "No," they were politely told by the sharemen that they intended to go with skippers who had motor-boats.

Of course, occasionally you will hear people complaining about the expense of motor-boats, but the man who complains does not understand the matter at all if he fails to see that the use of motor-boats adds thousands of quintals of fish to our catch every year, and the motor-boats, costly as they are, more than pay for themselves every time. Personally I know of no invention that has appeared in connection with our fisheries that has minimized labour for our men more than the motor-boat. Moreover, the fact that our common men, many of them without a word of learning, have become so proficient in handling these engines is astonishing. Another proof that the Newfoundlander can get there if he only gets a fair show!

Before leaving the codfishery laws, a word must be said about the repeal of the Bait Act.[3] The fact that the people on the south-west coast wished the Act repealed, and pointed out that would give many people a chance to earn a living and keep some of them off the dole did not surprise me in the least. But that the Commission responded to their wish and repealed the Bait Act for one year gave me the greatest surprise of my life. This surprise may be due to my having heard the arguments for and against; having given my vote in support of that measure forty-six years ago, and being still actively engaged in the interest and the welfare of the fisheries of today.

On my way to New York last May, shortly after the Bait Act was repealed at St. Pierre, we had on board as a passenger a Mr. Wareham from Harbour Buffett. In conversation with one of the French merchants at St. Pierre, he asked him what had become of the seventy fishing schooners they had fifty years ago. He said, "We lost them owing to the Bait Act, but we are going to get them back again now. The Government of Newfoundland has repealed the Bait Act and we will get plenty of bait from your people. We can get no bait at St. Pierre but plenty from Fortune Bay." On Saturday last, August 18th, I clipped the following from the *Daily News:*

"The Board of Trade of Newfoundland is presenting a Petition to His Excellency the Governor-in-Council, which contains the following: 'The Government of France is paying a bounty on salt codfish exported from France at $2.68 per cwt.' It is further pointed out that in addition to the above, the French Colony of St. Pierre pays another bounty which makes up altogether $4.69 per cwt. on large, $4.35 on medium, $4.24 on small."

It may be that nothing our Government has done or can do can alter that state of affairs, but I do think it was a great mistake to repeal an Act that has served us in good stead this last forty-six years. The Opposition of the day did not put one argument against the principle of the Act, but had no faith that the Government of the day had sufficient backbone to carry it out—an argument very often used by an Opposition against a Government on every question that arises.

I have before me a speech delivered by Mr. Morine (now Sir Alfred B. Morine): "With regard to the Bait Act I have only to say that if the Government really intended to enforce it, they should not have allowed the exportation of frozen herring to St. Pierre in American and Canadian vessels. If we on this side of the House believed that the Bait Act could be enforced so strictly that the French could not get bait at all, we would hold up both hands for the Bait Act." But the Act was passed and strictly enforced, and I have reason to believe was of more benefit to Newfoundland than any Act ever passed during the time we had responsible Government. The arguments of the Board of Trade today are similar to some of the arguments advanced by the trade of this country fifty years ago upon the same question, and it strikes me very forcibly that the repeal of the Bait Act would not have taken place had those in authority taken greater pains to study local conditions.

I now propose to discuss our herring laws. I shall deal with only one clause of the Regulations, that on page 77, Clause 27.

"Barring herring by any method is prohibited in all parts of the waters of Newfoundland, and in every case when a seine is used for the purpose of taking herring, it shall be hauled and tucked forthwith into boat or boats, and not from the shore or strand, except when the herring are required exclusively for bait."

For the last fifteen or twenty years a number of people who have written on our fisheries have always pitted us against Norway and Iceland; so much so that the Government of 1921 sent the late Hon. W. H. Penney to Norway. He brought back a very interesting report, from which I shall make a few relevant quotations. On page 19 he writes:

"I was much interested in watching this fishery because of the experience I had with herring in the Straits of Belle Isle quite a few year ago, when we enclosed thousands of barrels at a time with seines. I remember as well the action of our Fishery Board in forbidding the use of the seine, and the close season and other regulations enacted and enforced to protect our herring fishery, and still the herring practically forsook its old haunts along the Labrador and the Straits of Bell Isle and other centres along our coastline. I described the conditions as well as I could to the scientists of the Fishery Department and asked them for a reason as the desertion of the herring, but they could offer no opinion upon my statement of bare facts. I expressed my consternation at the practice in vogue in Norway, and I asked if similar conditions to ours were not anticipated. These men smiled at the suggestion, saying these conditions were continuing from year to year, and yet there was no diminution of the schools. Thousands of barrels of immature herring were taken and brought to the factories, where they were first boiled and the oil extracted, then pressed for the residue of oil and then ground into meal and guano. Herring of all quantities, all sizes are accepted at all seasons, and at points along the long coast-line factories are still in course of erection. I was informed those herring produced from 10 to 15 per cent. of their bulk in oil, and the fatter the herring the more acceptable are they. At first," he continues, "I was filled with a feeling of consternation and was regularly shocked to find that this valuable food fish was caught in this way for reduction at these factories, and I expressed myself along these lines, but I was told that I had the wrong idea altogether, that my idea was antiquated and not in keeping with the times. The argument was, why should fish capable of producing so many necessary articles, necessary to our civilization, and so much wealth, be allowed to come to our doors and no effort be made to utilize them. And," he adds, "I confess that I am now a convert to that idea and I believe I see here quite a source of wealth to the fishermen as well as good investment for capital. We prohibit the barring of herring; the Norwegians maintain it's the only way to get a No. 1 article, and give their reasons.

"In this connection I made inquiries as to the cure of Norwegian canned and pickled herring, and I was told that only herring taken with a seine and barred could produce the good No. 1 article. The herring should be confined in the seine for at least three days before being hauled out for cure. The reasons given for this were: the stomach of the herring must be emptied in order that the fish will keep and be of good flavour, and while enclosed for this length of time in the seine, the fish feed upon themselves, empty their stomachs, then the gill and heart alone are easily extracted, and as much of the blood as possible goes into the brine to keep the flavour of the fish soaking into it.

"This is exactly opposite to the course we pursue and we are continually asking the question: How is it that our herring cannot hold its own in the world's market, with the Norwegian and Scotch cure?"

When I was acting Minister of Marine and Fisheries I made the same investigation at Glasgow, Scotland. Up to that date we could never get our pickled herring to taste like the Scotch. On my arrival in Scotland I ordered a fresh herring for my breakfast. It was good, but no better than our Newfoundland fish. After breakfast I went to the Marine Department and found to my surprise that the Scotch handle their pickled herring in exactly the opposite way to ours. We were taught to wash the scales off and clean every drop of blood off. They, on the other hand, carry salt in their boats and sprinkle it on the herring so as to preserve the scale, and pack the herring in the barrel to preserve as much blood as possible.

That is one reason why I am seriously opposed to bleeding codfish while it is alive. This disposes of the herring fishery, except to say that since the herring has come under Government inspection and Government regulation, the price per barrel is so low that nothing can be made except by the owner, who makes his own barrel and puts that in as free labour. A vast difference from the time when we used to charter our vessels for Labrador herring and used to barter them in Canada—a barrel of herring for a barrel of flour.

A friend writing from Toronto recommends me to deal with the Labrador and shore fishery, also the seal fishery, its methods, its history and its many stirring incidents; the rise and fall of the sailing vessel industry, the rise and decline of the steam industry, and in the latter especially, the names and history of the leading ships such as the *Wolf,* the *Bear,* the *Neptune, Terra Nova* and many others. It may not be generally known today that while the cod fishery is 443 years old in Newfoundland, the seal fishery is only 138 years old, and the sealing industry in sailing vessels practically had its day and ceased to be during eighty years of this time. Many people attribute the decline of sailing vessels to steam, but nothing is further from the truth. As late as 1795 the total catch of seals for Newfoundland only amounted to 4,900. In these days the mode of prosecuting was by ice-boats. A great advance was made when small boats gave place to small schooners of from 30 to 50 tons, carrying 12 to 14 men. The first vessel my uncle commanded (he was master builder) was a full-rigged brigantine of 49 tons. The size of the vessel increased as the people gained knowledge and experience until brigs, and in some cases barques, of from 200 and 250 tons took the place of the 30- and 50-ton vessel.

The first method of catching seals was with nets. These nets consisted of a foot rope of about 2½ inch rope, a head rope of double-bank line with cork floats which kept the meshes open. It would be about 40 or 50 fathoms long and probably 10 feet in width. In 1795 the catch of seals was 4,900, mostly by nets. In 1804, 140 craft, averaging less than 30 tons each, with 1,639 men, caught 81,000 seals. During the year 1804, 35 shallops sailed from Conception Bay, and owing to the prevalence of northeast gales, 25 vessels were lost. The shallops appear to have all disappeared by 1806, and the seal fishery was then prosecuted in decked schooners. (Shallops was the name given to schooners without a deck.) Previous to 1800 the English and Irish prosecuting the cod fishery in Newfoundland returned home in the fall but when the ship seal fishery was started this population remained in the country and built up a permanent settlement. It changed the social habits of the people, as formerly the winter was a season of carnival, dancing, drinking and playing cards from house to house.

The seal fishery provided continual work for ships, carpenters and sail-makers, blacksmiths, builders, riggers, fitting out and repairing vessels, building boats, making oars, gaffs and everything connected with the business. There was a round of continual employment throughout the winter. The only let-up was at Christmas, when they would take three or four days off and sample one another's Christmas cakes and Christmas stock. One thing they were always sure of, if there was nothing strong they could always rely on spruce beer, for that was a beverage very common in those days. After a good day's work the body demanded that rest which is necessary for good health, and there was no time for that frivolity which seems to take us in hand when we have nothing else to do. I have reason to believe that when we built our own vessels for the seal fishery and cod fishery, we also built up a class of men who placed Newfoundland on the map. Many of them went into foreign countries and secured positions of eminence and responsibility. Others showed their true worth in the Great War.

Unfortunately, the mode of killing seals in the sailing vessels was very destructive, and although they commenced on a herd of seals that had been multiplying for ages, the fact remains that the 400 sailing vessels that we had in 1857 dwindled to 177 in 1866. The period during which the seals were destroyed runs between 1830 and 1857. It is recorded that in 1857 there were 400 vessels and 1,300 [sic; about 13,000] men engaged in connection with the seal fishery, and the number of seals brought in during that period is alarming in the extreme. During 10 years between 1830 and 1857 there were brought to port 5,270,193. There are 27 years between the dates that I have mentioned, but only 10 years are recorded. If the other 17 years not mentioned were as productive as the 10 years mentioned, it means that in 27 years the number of seals brought to port would be 14,000,000.

1 When bait was scarce jiggers were generally used because they do not require bait. A jigger consists of two or more hooks set in a bright lead sinker. The fisherman jerks the line rapidly up and down and curious cod are hooked. The big complaint is that many fish are hooked in the soft belly only to escape and die or become food for other cod fish.

2 Trawls were long lines with floats attached and stretched across a body of water. Numerous baited hooks on short lines hung from these main lines well below the surface. Fish, having bitten on these baited hooks, were thus caught. Trawls were more expensive than hand lines and jiggers but only needed to be attended to once or twice a day.

3 The Newfoundland Bait Act (and its amendments), generally speaking, prohibited the exportation of Newfoundland bait especially to St. Pierre and Miquelon. This measure was intended to reduce the French fishery and was largely successful. It was generally opposed by the exporters of bait in Fortune and Placentia Bay who viewed this trade as a valuable enterprise.

CERTIFICATE OF APPOINTMENT

MY SECOND COMMAND ON LABRADOR MAIL SERVICE

CHAPTER X

Sailing vessels—The dangers of sealing—Steamers—Raftering ice—A statistical survey—Close seasons—A codfish bounty—Agricultural prospects

We must now consider the methods used in these days in killing seals. If you had been called upon to sign an agreement in those days you would have found a clause to the effect that every man was to provide himself with a good gun and two locks, such as shall be approved of by the master, otherwise to be put upon the same footing as a batsman. What does this mean? I have no hesitation in saying that each vessel would carry 25 guns, but to be on the safe side we will suppose that each vessel had 20 guns. There is no record as far as I know as to the species of seals brought to port by the sailing vessels. Mr. Chafe does not give the species in his book before 1895, but, being conversant with sailing vessels (having sailed eleven springs in them), I estimate that the number of old seals brought to port would average at least 400 per vessel, or 160,000 per year. In my opinion, for every seal saved and brought to port 20 would be sunk.

Captain Jewer was fond of telling a story. When he asked a man how many seals he had killed that day, he replied, "I shot at 11, killed 10, sunk 6 and got 4." So that if you add the number brought to port to the number that was sunk you would sweep up the grand total to 15,000,000 — 2,000,000 more than the steamers brought in since they came to the country. Whereas it took the steamers 37 years to bring in 12,266,935, and the last of the 37 years was the first time they went over 300,000. Altogether, since the steamers came to the country (I am speaking now for 1921), they have, in 57 years, brought in 12,093,794 or 7,227,966 less than the sailing vessels brought in 47 years, and it is very remarkable that the largest number in any one years was in 1900, or 37 years after their advent in the country, and the next best year was 1910, just 47 years after their coming to the country, which to my mind is a poor argument to show that the seals have decreased because of the steamers.

Thus the history of the seal fishery in sailing vessels in this country lasted only eighty years, and to use a common expression, "they went up like a rocket, and came down like a stick." Scores of men who made thousands of dollars in the early forties lost them in the fifties and died poor men. In 1863 that great innovation, steam, took the place of sail in connection with the seal fishery, and claimed the right to its share of the loaves and fishes. Steam was by no means welcomed by those who had invested their money in sailing vessels, and had there been any chance of damning them out of existence, its stay would have been very short. Such, however, was not the case, and in a very few years it was realized that steam vessels had come to stay.

The first two vessels owned by Newfoundlanders were the first *Wolf* and *Bloodhound*. The *Bloodhound* was commanded by a Captain Graham, the *Wolf* by an uncle of mine, to whom I referred in the early pages of this book. The second year another ship was added, named the *S.S. Osprey*. Strange to say, for a number of years they met with poor success. Not until 1870 did ten ships reach 102,310 seals, and six of the ten steamers had made second trips for that year. A much superior class of steamer followed—the *S.S. Proteus*, the *S.S. Bear, Resolute, Neptune*. When these ships arrived we felt they were the last word in marine architecture, and it is only fair to say that these ships did good work. To the *S.S. Neptune* belongs the honour of bringing to port 1,000,000 in 53 years—during which time, however, she had eight masters.

To the late Mr. A. Harvey is due the credit of introducing the steel ship *S.S. Adventure*, a new type and with greater power; she left the other ships above-mentioned in her wake as they had left the sailing vessels, and held sway for three years from 1906 to 1909, when the *S.S. Florizel, Beothic, Bellaventure* and *Bonaventure* were added. In 1912 the *Stephano* and *Nascopie* appeared, two ships which surpassed anything that we could have imagined in our wildest dreams. Thus in 1906 we had 25 steamers and 4,051 men and in 1914 20 steamers and 3,959 men. One of the abuses which crept in, very largely through the politician, was the number of men who would be crowded aboard these steamers as crew. This not only made their quarters uncomfortable, but, with a load of seals, the crew would scarcely go over $30 per man.

In 1895, Captain Henry Dawe, M.H.A. for Bay Roberts, tried to pass a law to regulate the number in the crew of each vessel, but it was defeated by the politicians of that day. I tried it again in 1898 and succeeded, and had the proud satisfaction of seeing 1,400 men the past season averaging over $70 per man.

The seal fishery is very laborious work and some hundreds have given their lives in its service, yet there is not a master but refuses twice the number required for his crew each year. The number of deaths, according to Chafe's book, for sailing vessels in 50 years is 403, and for steamers in 51 years 318. The number of accidents in sailing vessels for 50 years is 15; the number of accidents in steamers in 51 years, 4. The steamer, however, carries many more men for a crew than sailing vessels. The *Southern Cross* had 173 in the crew, five times as many as the number in sailing vessels. Wireless is also a great prevention against accident. For instance, the *Greenland* disaster was caused by a lake of water between the crew and the ship. There was no wireless then, and the ship could not penetrate the jam she was in. The crew could not cross the lake but perished that night on the other side. Last spring my crew was caught in the same way; we could not cross the lake, my crew could not get over. I sent a wireless to Captain Blackwood of the *Imogene:* "My crew caught on the other side of a lake of water, we cannot get to them, will you please put them on the other side of the lake so that they can walk on board." He not only brought them on the other side of the lake but brought them right to my ship. To give my readers some idea of the quality of the *Imogene* as an ice-breaker,[1] I may point out that she can penetrate the ice at the rate of from three or four knots when the rest of us are jammed.

In this brief space I have attempted to outline the history of eighty years of sailing vessels in connection with the seal fishery, which are now as dead on the east coast of Newfoundland as if they had never existed. I do not think that anyone with a similar experience to mine wants to see them back again. They served their purpose for the first fifty years of the last century and developed some splendid men who are badly needed in connection with the work at the present time, but their place is filled today by a much improved class of boat, with far less hardships for the men. These boats are more in keeping with the times in which we live, and I see no more hope for the return of sailing vessels for the seal fishery than I have to see the wax candle or train oil lamps taking the place of gas or electric light.

The onward march of Progress cannot be stayed. We cannot afford retrograde measures. This, of course, does not mean that we must give ourselves up to every device that comes our way. Some people wax eloquent in telling us that we live in a machine age, and that one machine is doing the work of hundreds of men and doing it better and much quicker. They clamour therefore for the abandonment of the machine. Anyone can see that such a doctrine is detrimental to all modern reform, and would soon put us back to the same primitive style of doing things as our forefathers practised a thousand years ago. A much more helpful reflection is that the Creator is much greater than the creature. He creates, and that if the brain of man can create a machine, another brain working in another direction can contrive a plan whereby that machine can be so used to the true interest and happiness of mankind.

I now propose to survey the history of steamers; first the increase in size, and second, their decrease in number. Up to 1917 the smallest was the *S.S. Ariel*, 78 tons net, the largest the *S.S. Stephano*, 2,143 tons net, commanded by myself for three years and torpedoed by the Germans in 1916 off Nantucket lightship, and the *S.S. Erik* off St. Pierre. Altogether, since 1863, we have had eighty steamers in the Newfoundland seal fishery, four of which were lost in connection with the foreign service, ten were sold, six were returned to the foreign country, two were torpedoed, one, the *S.S. Seal*, was burnt at the seal fishery, five are now engaged at other work, eight are at present engaged at the seal fishery, forty-four were lost at that industry by natural causes, two of which—the two *Wolfs*—were lost by raftering ice. A word of explanation is necessary in connection with "raftering." Large sheets of ice, larger and thicker ice driven by the force of currents and wind will double up and smash smaller sheets. When this takes place, it is called "raftering." It is especially dangerous when the ice is in large sheets and comes in contact with land; when the ice is broken in small pans by the lift of a swell, there will be no raftering.

In 1896, when I lost the *Wolf,* the ice was raftered on the north side of Fogo Island and stuck fast to the land about eight miles off. There was a running joint which I managed to get in, and was working along in this joint. All the other ships behind me had tried to get in this joint but had failed, and I was ahead about fifteen miles, and that much nearer the seals. The day was calm and fine, and about the last thing you would think of was a rafter, but a large sheet driven by the force of the current caught us by the standing ice[2] and in less than twenty minutes the *Wolf* was a lost ship. Held, however, in the grip of the rafter, she could not sink although the water rushed in. This necessitated the drawing of the fires to prevent an explosion. The crew engaged in landing food on the ice, and also sails for the building of tents in case the wind should shift, the ice break and drive us out to sea. Fortunately, this did not take place, and about eight o'clock next morning when the tide turned and the ice loosened, the *Wolf* sank head first, smashing her topgallant mast and topgallant yards as they came in contact with the ice. Happily for us, we were on the standing edge that was fast to the land, and strapping our bags with as much of our belongings as we could carry, we walked ashore to Fogo.

My next experience with raftering ice was in 1924 in the *S.S. Terra Nova*. After the seals were pupped we had a succession of easterly winds which crammed all the ice in the bays and the young seals in White Bay. On the morning of departure, there was about three miles of ice crammed on the land. Outside lay open water. We commenced to butt our way into the water, and in less than an hour after leaving port, three of my men fell through a deceitful pan of ice and were drowned. It took us two days to reach the water, and then we steamed north in clear water and forced towards the land at White Bay until the ship jammed, unable to move. We then drove between the two Gray Islands, and with the aid of a westerly wind we entered White Bay and reached the whitecoats about 2:30 p.m.

My men returned at dark and reported panning 5,000. That night the wind varied to the east-north-east and blew a gale. Next morning we had breakfast at daylight and I was up to give my men their instructions for the day, remarking to my officers how well we had escaped raftering all through the spring. Suddenly I felt a nudge which I knew was a rafter. I dressed for the occasion for I knew it was stormy on deck. When I got on deck I met the doctor and one of my officers with their grips, leaving for the side of the ship. I was just about to stop them and upbraid them for their cowardice when, on reaching the bridge, I saw that about sixty of my crew, with their bags on the ice, had already left the ship. The ice was then coming over the rail, and it was not long before fourteen stanchions broke and the stanchions and rail were taken by the ice and lodged by the galley door. This continued until I imagined there were ninety tons of ice on her deck. I watched the masts to see that they were in line, and when the rafter stopped I heard from the engineroom that the ship was not taking a drop of water. I then called for silence, telling the crew that there was no fear of their lives, that the ship was not making a drop of water, and I named the masters of watch and gave them their work to do. By noon we had temporary repairs made, all the ice off deck, and after dinner the crew panned some 5,000 more seals.

The next day we were still held in the rafter, the ice broke about a mile from us and my men could not cross. I then ordered them to launch four dories up to the rent for the crew to cross to the other side, and to keep a crew with the dories in case other rents broke. That day we panned altogether 17,000 seals. After that we could not reach the seals and were still held in the rafter, being driven fifteen miles from our pans. At the end of the ninth day we got clear, reached our pans and picked up our 17,000 seals, and I don't know that we lost a single pan. Altogether we got 18,851.

Those who read these lines and know little about sealing will see that getting a million seals is not child's play and that the crews earn their money indeed.

I have said that in 1906 we had twenty-five steamers, and in 1914 we had twenty steamers prosecuting the seal fishery. Those who understood the work could see that the men who were putting money in this business were riding for a fall, but many of the investors thought they knew better. We were told that some of the men who were masters were too old for the work. They wanted younger men. That we old duffers were always going down the same old cow-path that our fathers used before us, and that every year we missed the seals. We were told that we left them to the south-east; all we wanted was an aeroplane to locate the different patches. The aeroplane arrived, but before it ever flew I gave a lecture in which I pointed out that in my opinion it would be useless. I was very guarded in my remarks, and told my audience that if I knew no more about the business than the landsmen, I thought I would favour the aeroplane. What was the

93

result? I make bold to say that the aeroplane cost us thousands of
dollars, and I challenge successful contradiction that it was ever
worth five dollars to us. To prove my case I have copied from
Chafe's book the list of trips every year we had an aeroplane and
the list of trips since 1929 when we discontinued using the
aeroplane.

1921	First year of aeroplane	101,452 seals
1922		126,031 "
1923		101,770 "
1924		129,560 "
1925		127,882 "
1926		211,531 "
1927		180,459 "
1928		227,022 "
1929		201,856 "
1930	No aeroplane out	241,236 "
1931		87,866 "
1932		48,613 "
1933		176,046 "
1934		227,390 "

And for the last two years I have not heard of a sound of seals
that we have left to the southeast.

A retrospective view of the industry is illuminating. For fifty
years we had manufacturing plants in all the principal outports.
In Harbour Grace, Munns, the owner of many steamers, finally
bought over by Crawford & Murray, St. John's, with eight sealing
plants reduced to two. In 1914 we could boast of twenty steamers
with 3,959 men; this year, 1934, of eight steamers with 1,499.
The contrast is great. At first glance it seems a case of how are
the mighty fallen! But on giving it more serious reflection one is
confronted with the fact that the two surviving plants are those

that have borne the burden and heat of the day, have met with very heavy losses and are still in the business. There is something, perhaps, in the law of the survival of the fittest!

Many have gone into this business with no experience and less money, whose only ambition was to get a share of the other fellow's work regardless of circumstances. This idea of "keeping up with the Joneses" is to my mind causing great financial harm. Although I do not gloat over the fact that in the last few years those who invested their money into the seal fishery lost it, I do suggest that if they had been wise they would have cut their losses rather than have invested more. First, on account of the decline in the number of seals. For while I do say there is no decline in the number of seals these last few years, the number of seals pupped on the east coast of Newfoundland does not average more than 200,000 per year, and to add to the number of ships and the number of men can only make matters worse.

The only year we have reached over 200,000 whitecoats since 1916 is 1934, when we reached 201,222. But with all our disappointments in connection with the seal fishery, I think I shall show that without it we would be infinitely worse off than we are. For since 1895, the first year Mr. Chafe gave values in his book, we have brought into this country in forty years 8,142,079 seals valued at $14,415,144.69, plus the number brought in by sailing vessels and motor schooners and landsmen. Another factor is that the seal fishery only lasts for two months in each year, and when you take into consideration the amounts paid the masters, the bounty paid cooks and officers, at least $8,000,000 has found its way into the pockets of the labouring people of this country at a time in the year in which they could not earn a dollar any other way.

After quoting the number brought in by steamers from 1863 to 1894, it is difficult to resist the conclusion, if one is not prejudiced against steamers, that there is no justification in the remark that steamers have destroyed the seals, or any justification for a close season. For the first thirty-two years after the advent of steamers, namely from 1863 to 1894, the steamers brought in 5,171,390 or an average of 161,605 seals per spring. For the last forty years the steamers averaged 203,327 seals per spring. Every year the steamers fall short of their average, and many people rise up in arms and say, "We told you so! The seals are getting killed out and unless the Government orders a close season the seal fishery will cease to exist." If one stops to think, statements of this kind are hopelessly out of date and superficial. For the sake of those who have prosecuted the seal fishery with me and formed a portion of my crew, I am giving the result of each voyage and the name of the ship, the number of seals and their value, and the amount per man according to Chafe's book.

		No. Seals	Value	Crew Bill	Crew
Wolf	1889	26,912	$55,141.20	$72.08	255
Second trip		4,561	—	—	—
	1890	16,068	35,908.38	45.89	261
	1891	25,237	48,633.00	62.35	260
Second trip		5,095	13,290.00	25.50	260
	1892	27,425	67,910.40	86.40	262
Second trip		5,054	13,290.00	25.50	262
	1893	9,174	21,610.74	26.49	272
	1894	5,742	11,164.35	14.15	263
	1895	30,290	40,907.54	53.75	272
	1896	Wolf lost			
Hope	1897	1,724	2,060.67	5.49	237
Aurora	1898	25,633	33,432.43	40.37	280
	1899	23,937	31,510.64	42.35	248
	1900	32,729	43,612.51	58.48	247
	1901	32,416	35,417.10	47.26	
	1902	24,184	34,343.02	44.02	249
Aurora	1903	26,069	35,364.57	62.37	260
	1904	34,849	45,811.65	81.22	187
	1905	4,553	7,870.44	13.97	187
Terra	1906	16,627	28,498.75	46.55	187
	1907	18,785	35,586.96	58.14	203
	1908	13,962	26,046.53	42.55	203

		No. Seals	Value	Crew Bill	Crew
Florizel	1909	30,488	$54,060.38	$88.33	203
	1910	49,070	90,800.19	148.36	270
	1911	28,129	40,818.97	50.20	270
Stephano	1912	13,110	24,929.32	30.66	270
	1913	37,882	69,562.09	85.56	270
	1914	22,210	48,112.55	59.17	270
Florizel	1915	2,592	5,932.75	7.35	270
					269
	1916	46,481	135,848.65	167.29	270
Terra	1917	23,313	62,948.00	101.94	204
	1918	20,295	110,300.96	178.47	205
	1919	12,568	47,729.06	76.12	150
	1920	3,660	22,466.25	36.35	150
	1921	10,754	17,761.82	39.20	150
	1922	23,157	36,180.74	74.90	160
	1923	14,241	31,360.50	65.74	160
	1924	18,851	36,075.20	74.68	160
	1925	18,215	42,736.27	80.48	160
	1926	22,529	51,740.47	107.12	160
Nascopie	1927	37,352	64,286.94	85.03	251
	1928	21,156	55,019.94	73.94	250
	1929	27,220	48,853.04	64.88	250
	1930	32,261	53,558.03	71.13	250
Thetis	1931	11,260	14,976.65	35.81	135
Terra	1932	9,157	11,680.97	26.13	149
	1933	11,410	12,626.88	26.91	155
Beothic	1934	48,701	68,580.97	101.04	225
	Total	1,007,100	$1,926,288.36	$642,096.12	11,209

Add to this the amount 700 in a sailing vessel and 300 not on specification one year in *Aurora,* and it brings my total up to 1,008,100.

Every one of my crew who reads these lines will be reminded of the part he played in establishing a world's record, and I take this opportunity of thanking them for the splendid work which they performed.

Now in dealing with close seasons, I cannot help saying that it seems to me that the people who talk so glibly of close seasons either fail to understand the question or are indifferent to it. That may seem an abrupt way of putting it, but let me try to qualify what I mean. These people have not studied the thing sufficiently to know that we have been having close seasons all the time. In other words, nature herself has provided a close season, or the Newfoundland seal fishery would have long been a thing of the past. Hatton & Harvey's "History of Newfoundland" gives an account of the first close season, so far back as 1817, a little over twenty years from the time it started. They say: "The spring seal fishery was a failure, and I could give lots of other springs before ever we had steamers when we had close seasons. The spring of the Wadmans, the spring known as the spring of the wrecks; 1865, known as the spring of Green Bay; later still, 1915, when only 47,004 were brought in by the combined fleets, seven of them being our most powerful icebreakers; again, in 1920, when the total number brought in was 33,989, and again in 1932, only 48,613." Only those who, for the last fifty years, have been taking the bitter with the sweet, understand what the close seasons, provided by an unseen hand, have meant, and only those with almost unlimited capital behind them have been able to stand the strain. They have to be able to do so at all because in some years they have been fortunate.

If a Government orders a close season for a number of years, they are not able to recoup for the close season provided by Providence or whatever you may call it. In such a contingency, I for one would not be surprised if the people who have taken such chances in the past put up their shutters with the evident intention of not taking them down again. Furthermore, it is worthy of note that the close season provided by nature is not so hard on the common people as the close seasons provided by law, for in all the close seasons the people have been provided with two months' food and crops[3] to the value of $9 cash to each man, the losses each time having been borne by the outfitter. If the Government orders a close season it would mean that some two thousand men would be out of employment without credit for two months. On reflection, perhaps, we should "better bear the ills we have that fly to those we know not of."

Hatton & Harvey, in their remarks on the failure of the seal fishery in 1817, speak of it from another standpoint altogether than the one on which I would like to made a few remarks. At that time the inhabitants of Newfoundland numbered only 70,000 [sic; the number may have been closer to 40,000], and those in authority had proposed the removal of the inhabitants from the country. This was not the first time they had proposed the deportation of the settlers. In 1670 the merchant owners and ship masters and the inhabitants of the western part of the kingdom petitioned the King (Charles II) that the inhabitants of Newfoundland and their families, then amounting to 3,171, should be removed to Jamaica, St. Christopher, or some other of His Majesty's plantations.

Now, in 1817, the population of the country being 70,000, it was actually proposed that they be removed as the means of their own relief.[4] The Committee of the House of Commons, naturally enough, inquired whether the fisheries were insufficient for their support, since a portion of the inhabitants could not find profitable employment in the cultivation of the soil. The reply made by witness after witness was that the agricultural improvement of Newfoundland was utterly impracticable, and only one merchant urged the encouragement of agriculture as a remedy for the poverty of the people. The result was that no effort was made to open up the country for agricultural settlement, and the matter was left on a *laisser-faire* basis.

I regret to say that from our leading men of today, agriculture is not receiving much encouragement, and too many of our leading men are talking of a bounty on codfish, which, in my opinion, is most uneconomical and suicidal to our best interests.

It is also recorded that at the very time when they were trying to depopulate the country, the local authorities in Massachusetts were giving a bounty for each Newfoundland fisherman brought into the state. How utterly unfounded were their representations regarding the sterility of the soil and the severity of the climate, appears from the fact that eighteen years afterwards, in 1836, notwithstanding the disadvantages of the soil, the census gave the value of our annual produce as £191,234 for the land under cultivation.

In the census of 1845 the estimated value of land then under cultivation and of agricultural stock is given at £677,040, or equal to $3,385,000. In fact, wherever ordinary skill and industry have been exercised in the clearance and cultivation of the soil, it has never failed to repay the labour expended on it. The agricultural population of Newfoundland is more comfortable and independent than that exclusively engaged in the fisheries. Before leaving this subject I would like to quote from Mr. Alexander Murray, an authority on the question. He states as far back as 1864: "It can be no longer doubted that Newfoundland now presents a promising field for mining enterprises, and it contains enough of fertile land to sustain in comfort a population of several millions of people." Yet seventy-four years after these words are spoken we are still quibbling over the question with thousands of our people in want and fed on the dole, and thousands of acres of agricultural land waiting for a plough to open it up. Even the efforts put forward some time ago by the L.D.A. have not brought what some of us hoped for.

There is comfort in the reflection, however, that the Commission Government are doing something on these lines, and it is well to remember how difficult it is for them to do more than it is already doing. The spirit is willing but finances are weak, and to bring about the desired results, in my opinion, millions of money will be required and thousands of men will have to be employed. While we cannot expect such a work to be accomplished in a year or two, the quicker the foundation is laid the sooner can we hope for recovery from the stranglehold which grips us today. Be that as it may, one fact seems to me to be inescapable, that is, that we can never hope to retrieve our fallen fortune by the fisheries of this country alone. Big catches will mean a low price and the people will never be able to pay their bills; small catches or blanks will mean that history will repeat itself. Some of the people will have to be fed, or revolts will take place as in the past. Whenever that has happened, it has been a losing battle for the Government in power.

Yesterday morning when I went downtown I met a young man who is in charge of a mercantile business. "I see you report a large catch of fish on Labrador?" he observed. I said, "Yes." "Captain So-and-So thinks you are wrong." "Well," I replied, "perhaps that captain is giving you what he thinks you want. I am giving you the truth." He replied, "Well, we don't think it does us any good in the foreign markets to report a large catch." I might have given my opinion on that to one of the papers and perhaps stirred up a newspaper controversy. I thought I had better give my opinion here, and to me it seems preposterous at this time in the world's history, when we have news travelling under water, through water, on the land, and through the air, that we should attempt to keep the report of our fishery to ourselves and keep ourselves so much out of touch with other countries who are spending hundreds of thousands of dollars in news bulletins. This man gave me his reason as to why he thought we should not tell the truth when we had a big catch; it was that the foreign markets, hearing we had a big catch, would lower the price. But is not that all the more reason why we should tell them the truth all the time? Let us suppose for argument's sake that we can manage to mislead them for this year. How can we reasonably hope for the same people to believe us next year? That is, however, the line of business that some people pursue all the time until they become so notorious that nobody will trust them or take their word.

A homely illustration will perhaps make my meaning clearer. On one side of the Board of Trade Room in St. John's, there is a blackboard containing prices of wheat, corn, oats, pork, ribs, lard, cotton, from Chicago, Winnipeg, Liverpool and places in Canada. On the other side is a blackboard indicating the quantity of fish in Oporto, Norway and Vienna, and the consumption each week. As soon as the Norway and Iceland fisheries commence we secure the daily number and a comparison with the same date last year. This man says in effect, "That's all right and it serves us a good turn, but we don't intend to run our business on these lines; what we have we hold. We intend to keep them in the dark and make them believe we only have a small catch until we can get them to pay us a good high price for the greater part of it, anyway." Let it suffice to say that there is a body of well-informed opinion on the other side.

George W. Perkins says: "Each day it becomes more and more apparent that all questions in this country must be settled before the bar of public opinion. If our laws regulating large businesses provide for proper and complete publicity so that the labour of a concern will know what is doing, so that the stockholders will know what is being done, and the public will have as much information as either—many of our present difficulties will disappear. In place of publicity being an element of weakness to a business concern, it will be an element of strength."

Today I was speaking to a young man who, a short time ago, was in Halifax trying to sell some fish, and he very pleasantly took me to one side and said, "I was mad enough with you the other day in Halifax to bite your head off."

"For what reason?" I inquired.

He said, "For that report you brought up off the Labrador."

I said, "My report was the truth, and if you don't want the truth then don't send me to make up the report."

"Wait till I tell you," was his reply. "I was with a merchant in Halifax trying to sell him some fish the day before your report came out and almost had the deal finalized, and he asked me to call and see him tomorrow morning at ten o'clock. On my way down next morning I bought the *Halifax Herald*, and there in

great flaring headlines was 'Fish eating the rocks on Labrador.'"
I said, "But that was not my report." "No, but that is what the papers said."

"You surely don't hold me responsible for all the papers say," I protested.

"Well," he said, "I put the paper in my pocket and went on to the office of the merchant on Water Street. As soon as I entered the office the merchant said to me, 'Did you see the paper this morning, the fish eating the rocks on Labrador! That's Captain Kean's report.' He said, 'I know that man and you can always rely on what he says.'"

I wish I could pay the same compliment to every man in business in Newfoundland, but I am afraid that what the Scotsman said about some of them would be more in keeping with their line of conduct: "I said in my haste all men are liars." Faith, if he lived today, he might say it at his leisure. What this young man thought was that my truthful report was hindering him from making a good sale of his fish. Nobody can blame him for trying to make a good sale; that is natural, but what he was really up against was the law of supply and demand.

That law was in existence before either he or I was born; it is at the root of every business transaction, whether we like to admit it or not. The merchant may have been ready to lay hold on my report to secure the best possible price for himself and the young man may have blamed my report for not getting a better price for his fish, but had I never been born the business man in Halifax would nevertheless have known enough about the lay of supply and demand to offer him exactly what he did that day. But what was the final result? Notwithstanding my report, that young man sold more fish in Nova Scotia while he was there that I have heard of in the same length of time, not on account of my report, not on account of his good looks, which may have helped him somewhat, but on account of a scarcity of fish in Nova Scotia.

What arguments do these people use who try to contradict my report that from Battle Harbour to Domino the fish were not so good? There was always more salmon caught on this part of the coast than farther north, and this year when the fishing folk arrived, codfish was plentiful. However, the people worked at the salmon, and although they did not get so many salmon as last year, the small supply created a larger demand, so that financially they were just about as well off. In this report I was governed by the advice given me by parties interested in that business, and before dispensing with this subject I want to point out the relationship between the report I gave and the standpoint of the people who have attempted to contradict it. One of the latter was the captain of a steamer interested in the salmon business who calls on two or three ports and who must be governed by the reports given him from two or three persons. Others may have made a casual visit to Labrador and only know what they are told.

I was on the *Kyle* seeking information for the Department of Fisheries. Captain Clark of the *Kyle* would always stop his ship whenever he saw a motor-boat coming for news. Whether it were morning, noon or night, I was at hand and would take the most reliable man I could find and take a list of the trips. I would make a note in a book which I have now in my possession and which anyone is at liberty to examine. Moreover, I copied all the trips in my correspondence to Mr. Fudge, the Chief Fishery Officer. Although that gentleman is reputed to have said that he does not think the voyage will be as great as last year, I am satisfied to wait for results. In speaking to one of our large supplying merchants the other day I said, "What report do you get from your schooners?"

He said, "Well, a great many of them are home, they are all loaded. I have not heard of one blank, have you?"

I said, "No, not one." Some, no doubt, who read this will think I am labouring the question. My only reason for doing so is that I am a great believer in truth, and I do believe it essential to the welfare of this country to teach our young people to be honest and truthful.

If you have been in Court, and the Judge has asked, "Guilty or not guilty?" you may have heard the prisoner at the Bar say,

"Not guilty." A distinguished lawyer has perhaps appeared for the prisoner and informed the Judge that he wants to alter his plea of "Not guilty" to "Guilty" when he has heard sufficient evidence to convict his prisoner. He will then, of course, use all his efforts to mitigate the sentence, perhaps because the prisoner has a mother or a wife and children depending upon him for support. You may admire the ability of the lawyer in defence of his client and the leniency of the Judge in mitigating the sentencing, but what hope can you have for a country if the majority of the people have no more regard for their word than the prisoner I have just described?

Why, then, this comment on my report from Labrador? It amounts, I submit, to nothing more nor less than that I dared to tell the truth of the reports that were given to me from the fishermen themselves. It is perhaps fitting to leave this topic with the words of Charles Summer: "I honour any man who, in the conscious discharge of his duty, dares to stand alone; the world with ignorant, intolerant judgment may condemn; the countenances of relatives may be averted, and the hearts of friends grow cold; but the sense of duty done shall be sweeter than the applause of the world, the countenance of relatives or the hearts of friends."

1 The *S.S. Imogene* was the best ice-breaker/sealer ever to operate in the Newfoundland seal fishery.

2 Standing ice is ice that remains firmly in position, sometimes attached to land. Running ice is ice that moves, sometimes quite rapidly.

3 The crop was the name given to the supplies issued to the men, upon request, before the voyage. Men who so wished could purchase items (knives, mitts, goggles, etc.) to a total value of $9. At the end of the voyage $12 was deducted from the sealer's income. If the voyage was a total failure the $9 crop was forgiven.

4 The actual proposal requested the removal of about 5000 people.

ABRAM KEAN'S FAMILY. FRONT: L-R: ABRAM KEAN, CECIL, ALFREDA, JOSEPH W., BERTHA, CAROLINE YETMAN KEAN (WIFE). STANDING, L-R: SAMUEL G., NATHAN, AND WESTBURY. DOG: GYP PHOTO: COURTESY OF MADELINE (KEAN) GOSSE.

CHAPTER XI

Floating schooners and cod—A bird's-eye view of the situation—
Pure food laws—The railway

In previous chapters in this book I have shown the rise and fall of the herring fishery, the rise and fall of sailing vessels in connection with the seal fishery, and the rise and fall of steamers in connection with the seal fishery. I now propose to deal with floating schooners in connection with the cod fishery. Unfortunately there are no statistics further back than 1923, and the following figures will illustrate our position in 1923 and our position up to 1934.

Date	Vessels	Men engaged as crews
1923	345	2,407
1924	396	2,790
1925	497	3,695
1926	463	3,487
1927	358	2,671
1928	385	2,768
1929	409	3,010
1930	398	2,992
1931	358	2,723
1932	303	2,303
1933	274	2,108
1934	341	2,637

The above figures show that we have not held our own in comparison with the number of vessels employed twelve years ago. When one investigates the matter further, a much more discouraging state of things in connection with our floating vessels is revealed. Many of the vessels were not built in this country but bought from Nova Scotia at about one-eighth of their original cost. Why? Because at the low price of fish it would never have paid to have had new schooners built. Many of our leading men, who noticed how our Labrador schooners were falling off, thought to remedy the matter by offering a higher bounty for shipbuilding. Every time that arose during the time I was in the Legislative Council I was deadly opposed to it on the ground that if a man could not pay his bills and get a new schooner when his old one was worn out, higher bounty would not remedy matters.

A comparison between the number of shipbuilding plants in this country fifty years ago and the number of shipbuilding plants today answers the question. The thought of building new schooners for the fishery on two-dollar fish is too serious to contemplate. The schooners mentioned in the table which I have submitted above range from 30 to 120 tons; I am now going to speak of a much smaller class, namely of from 15 to 20 tons. They have practically become obsolete except perhaps at Placentia, St. Mary's and Fortune Bays where, if I mistake not, the number has considerably decreased this last thirty years. The 20-quintal boats that were in the northern bays are almost forgotten, motor-boats having taken their place.

Larger schooners and larger crews are taking the place of the 40 and 50-ton schooners of forty years ago, and it is for this reason that with four schooners less than in 1923 we are carrying 233 more men. It makes no difference to whom you are speaking, whether it is the skipper of a 120-ton schooner or the skipper of a 50-ton schooner, they are all of the same opinion—one cannot continue long with any hope of making it pay on two-dollar fish. I want it to be distinctly understood that I am not now suggesting that the price of Labrador fish is two dollars when it ought to be three, but I am taking it for granted that the trade cannot afford to give more, having regard to the law of supply and demand.

Prior to 1800 an English ship fishery was conducted in Newfoundland, but the competition of the shore men in the colony destroyed the ship fishery. Will the same thing happen in Labrador? It became clear that shore men could sell their fish at a lower price than ship men. Is there anything in the situation to negate the argument applied to Labrador? Might not the solution of present unemployment of fishermen be solved to some extent by aiding their migration from parts of Newfoundland to parts of Labrador? As I have dealt partly with that subject in a previous chapter, there is no need for me to repeat myself, except to say that since I wrote on the subject I have spoken to Captain Dalton who was up to North-West River in Hamilton Inlet. He told me that he had a most beautiful dinner there, and the only two things on the table that did not grow there were salt and flour. I think that will equal anything we have here in Newfoundland. He also told me that there were eighty-four families living there, and there was not a single case of drawing the dole there last winter.

I never had much faith in the gold on Labrador, but I do believe from what I have seen this summer from Port Hope Simpson and St. Mary's River and from what I hear about North-West River, that we may hope in the near future to see many of our unemployed move to Labrador, where they and their families will be much more comfortable than they can ever hope to be in Newfoundland. This will only be history repeating itself, for the early settlers of this country were people from England, Ireland and Scotland, who were forced by circumstances to leave the land of their birth and look for occupations for themselves.

Today I received the history of our Banking fleet for the last ten years:

Date	Schooners	Crew
1924	36	607
1925	41	753

Date	Schooners	Crew
1926	47	872
1927	41	740
1928	51	932
1929	56	1,033
1930	62	1,150
1931	50	966
1932	46	844
1933	51	919

This shows a slight improvement in comparison with the figures for our Labrador fleet, but there is still no cause for self-congratulation, particularly when you take into consideration the amount of money spent on the south-west coast for bait freezers, principally for the Bankers, at the country's expense. What then is the lesson to be learned from the figures which I have quoted? If we are wise we will learn our lessons as other countries have done, namely, that fishing in schooners cannot pay with cheap fish. Before referring to other countries I must indicate that some of our people have learned their lesson and profited by altering their methods of fishing. Yesterday I received official figures from the authorities of the Railway. They show that the Coastal boats carried upwards of three thousand fishermen from Conception Bay, Trinity Bay, Bonavista Bay, on to the so-called French shore, including Gray Islands, browse Fishott Islands, Quirpoon and Cook's Harbour, farther up the Straits and Labrador. Hardly any of these places were ports of call when I first ran the *S.S. Portia* and *Prospero*. Many of the people stationed at these places were at one time masters of schooners at the fisheries, found it could not pay and abandoned that mode of fishing.

About thirty or forty years ago St. Pierre had seventy fishing schooners; now she has none. Hundreds of that beautiful type of schooner built and manned by Nova Scotians which used to ply on the banks and shores on Labrador have practically vanished, and a splendid fleet from Gloucester is supplanted by what are now called speed boats, mainly used to supply fresh fish to Boston and other markets in the United States. A friend of mine who was there recently told me that it is useless for us to look to markets for our salt codfish in the United States. Their mode of living and their customs are vastly different from the European, and I am inclined to believe him.

Having come to this conclusion, it for us to consider what we can do to improve our modes of fishing and meet the competition in the foreign markets. It is hardly fair to say that Governments in the past have not tried to do something. Especially is this true of the Government which last year voted itself out of power, led by the Hon. F. C. Alderdice. They did a bold stroke of business by declaring that the time had come when something should be done to remedy the existing state of affairs. It was pointed out that our fishermen were handling our fish as an article of food, and that the fishermen should lead the way by taking more care in washing it from the knife and generally taking greater precautions. It was further stated that fish was sent to market by our exporters that could not compete with our foreign competitors and that we were losing our markets. How are we going to reclaim them? By making it compulsory that all fish for foreign markets should be inspected by Government inspectors.

An Act embodying these principles was passed by the Legislature. Where could we get a man? As usual, the need brought forth the man. A Mr. Davies, who was for some time a school teacher and a Government analyst in this country, was chosen for the position. When the question was asked, "What does this man know about the fisheries?" we were told that there were to be two other men associated with Mr. Davies and that these two men would do the groundwork, with Mr. Davies as the final arbiter. In due course Davis was appointed, but not the other two men. Davies was head of the Salt Codfish Board, with absolute control of appointments and dismissals. Being of a genial disposition he ruled well, but not long, unfortunately for us. Mr. Davies had a call to come up higher. Like a wise man he obeyed, and we were left like sheep without a shepherd. The Chief Inspector appointed under Mr. Davies was told by the Commission that the Salt Cod-fish Board would be dissolved at the end of June, and that in future all laws governing the fisheries were to come within the province of the Department of Natural Resources. Following that, Rules and Regulations were drawn up and issued. One on the 2nd of June, the other on the 16th of June, the plainest and best that it was ever my lot to see. One of these clauses contains the following:

"The Government intends to enforce rigidly a strict cull on the Culling Board, and only fish which measures up to the standard defined by the Government will be permitted to be exported as No. I."

Rule No. 8 from the Department of Natural Resources contains the following:

"See that beaches are protected by fences and flakes raised a sufficient height from the ground to avoid the possibility of animals trampling the fish and soiling the beaches and flakes.

"Fish in fagots or piles should be protected from heavy dews and rains with covering, and when dried and ready for market must be kept in clean snug stores, whose doors should not be opened during periods of damp or wet weather."

Both of these clauses are so well drafted that is reminds us of some of the laws made during the time we had responsible government, and most people seemed satisfied when the letter of the law could be found upon our Statute Book, even though everybody knew that these laws were more honoured in the breach than in the observance. It is very evident by the last report of the Commission that someone is disturbed over losing the talqual system. Here is what it says:

"It was particularly difficult to frame a regulation forbidding the existing custom of purchase talqual. Evidently the Department feel that they are on the horns of a dilemma and dare not hold on or let go."

I have been engaged under the Salt Cod-fish Act and this year by the Department of Natural Resources. If I am asked whether I see any prospect of improvement, I say, "Yes, the fishermen have responded nobly in my opinion. Never in the history of my time did the fishermen look after their fish better and produce a better article in salt bulk than they have in the last two years." I am speaking now of Labrador, but on my way home last night one the foremen in one of the exporters' stores told me that the same thing was true on the southern shore. When it comes to the making of the fish, however, I cannot, unfortunately, report so favourably, the absence of covering or suitable stores or flakes is very evident, but it is only fair to say that there are exceptions. Baine Johnston's place at Battle Harbour is in good condition, and Venison Island, Fishing Ships Harbour, Comforts Bight, Indian Harbour and probably Horse Harbour and Smokey are also exceptions.

Dogs roving at large are most provoking, and in my opinion unsanitary. To my mind, the Department of Natural Resources should at once issue instructions for next year to the effect that all dogs and animals must be pounded up or fenced in before fish-making takes place, otherwise all this talk about pure food laws under prevailing conditions is but a tragic farce.

Down to the previous paragraph, I have not offered my opinions but restricted myself to facts which are stubborn things. My opinion, for what it is worth, briefly amounts to this. The less Governments interfere in matters of business, the better. I was always opposed to restraint in trade, but I do think it is the duty of a Government to insist on pure food laws being maintained, and all I have attempted to do, and the advice I have given the last two years has been with this object. If the Department of Natural

Resources can enforce laws in connection with the curing and making of fish so that a better quality can be produced and the exporters can purchase from the fishermen without any interference from the Government, meanwhile maintaining the principle of pure food laws, then that is the better way. If, on the other hand, the principle of pure food laws cannot be maintained, then whatever stands in the way must go, whether it is the talqual system or the insistence on all fish being inspected for foreign markets. We must prove to the outside world that what we export from this country in the way of foodstuffs has received that care and attention that is necessary for a favourable comparison with all other countries in the world, and all the more because we form a part of the British Empire which has already accomplished so much in that direction.

Before closing this chapter I should like to say how pleased I was to hear the last report from the Railway that we may look forward in the near future to the time when the Railway will be an asset instead of the liability that it has so far been. From its inception to the present time, it has been a bone of contention with all Governments, and, although one Government after another has taken it in hand for reform each succeeded in leaving the situation worse than its predecessor, that is until the Cashin and Monroe Government came into power. Then an effort was made to place it under control of our local talent, and if there is one man in the country who should be deservedly proud of the latest report of the Railway, it is Judge Higgins of the Supreme Court, who was at the time representing the district of St. John's East. He had worked for a long time at the Railway and knew the value of the men whose cause he was championing. He never minced matters one little bit but made the Legislative Hall ring, calling by name such men as Herbert Russell, Joyce, Pittman and others.

I have never been a shouter for local talent at any cost, neither am I opposed to other nationalities coming amongst us as long as they settle down among us and help to build up some trade or industry; so far as I am concerned the door is ever on the latch for all such people, but I am proud to feel that we have such local men in charge of our railways as Herb. Russell of Musgrave Harbour, Manager; Captain Dalton, from the Marine Department from Pool's Island, Bonavista Bay (where a lot of other good men come from); Joyce in the Engineering Department, from Carbonear; Mr. Pittman, the genial Passenger's Agent from St. John's, and others from the remote parts of Newfoundland, all working in the interest of one common cause to make the Railway and Coastal boats paying investments for this country.

They have proved to the world what hundreds of their fellow countrymen have done before them in the last hundred years, namely, that whenever Newfoundlanders get a fair show, they show the world that they can play their parts with all comers. Their trains and coastal boats go and come with a regularity by which you can almost set your watch. Information is given at the dispatching office in such a way as to convey the idea that the truth is not something to withhold from the general public as was the case in the distant past. In offering the entire staff my hearty congratulation, I feel certain I am expressing the sentiments of a large number of the travelling public who travel on the Newfoundland Railway and Coastal boats.

KEAN FAMILY PORTRAIT: FRONT: CAPTAIN ABRAM KEAN, WESTBURY, BERTHA, CECIL, AND CAROLYN (YETMAN) KEAN. BACK: JOSEPH W., ALFREDA, NATHAN, AND SAMUEL G. PHOTO: COURTESY OF MADELINE (KEAN) GOSSE.

CHAPTER XII

The Commission Government—The Empire Marketing Board—
Scientific ideas—Caribou and moose hunting—Whaling—"Back
to the Land"—Mackerel and lobster—The squid

In discussing our Commission Government I must state at the outset that they are to be congratulated on the publicity which has attended their activities. The House of Assembly in the past was open to all, but the real business of the country was done by the Executive Government behind closed doors, and the country was not aware of may of the things that were transacted there. The Government party, also behind closed doors, was made aware of what the Executive intended to do; if it did not meet with the approval of the Governing party, it would be turned down in party meeting. If it met with the approval and consent of the Government party, it would be brought into the House of the peoples' representatives and then, no matter what arguments were brought forward by the Opposition, it would be carried by a strict party vote.

That is why in the past we have seen so many laws passed one year and amended the next year, some of them repealed altogether and others remaining on our Statute Book as a dead letter, and on occasions when the laws have been consolidated, many have been dropped altogether. The following appears in the record of the business transacted by our Commission of Government yesterday:

"The Fishery Research Commission constituted in 1930 principally for the purpose of controlling the Fishery Research Laboratory at Bay Bulls was abolished, as the Laboratory is now under the direct supervision of the Department of Natural Resources. The Commission consisted of seven persons, four of whom were nominated by the Empire Marketing Board, which at the time shared half the cost of the Laboratory's operations, and three nominated by the Newfoundland Government. The total expense of the Laboratory is now borne by the Newfoundland Government."

If I mistake not, the whole of the Bay Bulls plant was the product of the Prime Minister of Newfoundland's activity in 1930, and in my opinion, this man was as much in earnest as he ever was in his life when he succeeded in getting the Empire Marketing Board to share that enterprise with the Newfoundland Government. The fact that the Empire Marketing Board was the first to withdraw from that enterprise is proof that to them, at least, all is not gold that glitters.

That some of us had no faith in future results is not worth discussing here, but to show that I am not afraid to face any arguments that the supporters of the Bay Bulls plant may put forward, I am going to ask the Commission of Government to carry on the good work they have so well begun. Publish the entire cost of the Bay Bulls Station, what it has cost the Empire Marketing Board, what it cost Newfoundland, and then the benefits we have derived from it! The friends of the Bay Bulls enterprise will perhaps suggest that this is impossible because they are working for a future, and it may be that it will take a hundred years before they will be able to show results. That being so, why then have the Empire Marketing Board dropped out? Is not the explanation perhaps that these people began to build and were not able to finish?

Although I am writing this, I want it to be understood that I am on the best of terms with the Principal and others of the Bay Bulls enterprise as well as a friend of some of the well-wishers of

118

TEMPLET ALLENPAUL

EXECUTIVE CLASS/CLASSE AFFAIRES

ETKT0142182630473

Flight/Vol

AC 125 28APR

From/De

ST JOHNS NL   Frequent Flyer/Voyageur assidu

AC*E

Boarding Time/Heure d'embarquement **12 : 10**

d 1245 x 1490

Departure Time/Heure de depart 12:45

Airline Use/A usage interne 0101 YYT65645

Destination

TORONTO-T1

Gate/Porte **3**   Seat/Place **03A**

Boarding Pass | Carte d'accès à bord

2851

TEMPLET A

Cabin/Cabine

J

Flight/Vol

AC 125

TORONTO-T1

Seat/Place

03A WINDOW/HUBLOT

Remarks/Observations

AIR CANADA

that plant, and on one occasion when I was asked to move a vote of thanks to the Principal, Dr. Thompson, I expressed myself that in my opinion for the work of the Bay Bulls plant to be of interest to Newfoundland, it was necessary for the scientist and the practical man to get together and discuss matters. I am of the same opinion still. One can no more ignore the ideas of the practical man of this country in connection with the fisheries and expect success than one can ignore the scientific side and expect a similar result. If the practical masters of the sealing fleet could have been easily persuaded they would have gone to the southeast when they left St. John's to look for seals for the last twenty years, instead of the north, as their better knowledge dictated to them.

I do not wish, in anything I may say, to make it appear that I am not a believer in science or that I do not appreciate the rapid strides that science is making, but it is well to remember that science has not always brought peace and contentment or happiness to this world or its people. Submarines and gas bombs, powerful machine-guns, aeroplanes and many other destructive weapons are the products of science, and the League of Nations was established at a cost of millions of dollars to the nations of the world in an attempt to reach an agreement whereby these destructive weapons may never be used again in the destruction of life and property as they have in the past. The *S.S. Daisy*, which is in the Government service, is also the product of science, and under the captaincy of Captain Dalton, took two Commissioners and others of their staff from here to Labrador in a few days, and during that time travelled over sixteen thousand miles of ground. A marvellous development of science. In this year of grace 1934, when science is at its peak, the whole world seems more concerned than ever before with the problem of giving the people employment and keeping them from starving. Evidently, therefore, it requires something more than science to get us right.

The second paragraph in the Commissioner's report reads as follows:

119

"The Commissioner for Natural Resources reported that up to date his Department had disposed of 2,600,000 pounds of salt bulk fish at 1 1/2 cents per pound f.o.b. Labrador, and 4,000 quintals of Labrador soft cure at prices which will net fishermen on the Labrador $2.50 and $2 per quintal for first and second quality respectively."

Prices obtained for shore fish averaged $4 a quintal first quality, Spanish realized up to $7.50 per quintal. No doubt the Commission regret with many of us that they cannot pay a better price to the fishermen for their Labrador fish, but it represents the highest I have yet heard quoted. From what I have heard so far, one of our fish-making plants paid $2.20 per quintal and charged 30 cents per quintal fish-making, which it net to the fishermen $1.90. Another plant is taking $2.25 with 30 cents fish-making which will mean $1.95. The fact that they have published this is in striking contrast to the practice of past Governments, which voted hundreds of thousands of dollars and spent it among their friends, the first knowledge the public had of it being when the public accounts were tabled in the House of Assembly.

The next paragraph contains the fact that the Commissioner for Natural Resources has decided to issue permits to hunt caribou and moose during the coming winter months. These permits will be distributed through magistrates and relieving-officers; a limited number being allotted to each relieving-officer, who will be instructed to grant permits only to those in need of food. A condition of the permit will be that while a portion of the animal will be allowed to the person who shoots it, the rest will be distributed by the magistrate, relieving-officer or constable, to needy residents of the district. This measure will, I think, be approved by every right-thinking person, who must certainly know many of the outlying settlements, where for want of proper nourishment many of our people are suffering from beri-beri, and to deny them proper food for the sake of providing sport for their better-off neighbours is, to my mind, most ridiculous. Some will object and say, "What are you going to do if you destroy all your deer and moose?" My answer is, "Just about the same as we are doing as long as we provide a close season and not permit them to be killed." It is most remarkable, however, what sticklers we have in this country for close seasons.

A few years ago when the Norwegians came out here to hunt whales, the whales were very plentiful. The first companies to put money in whaling met with great success, and as the number of whalers increased the opposition to whalers commenced also. We were told that unless the whalers were stopped our cod fishery would be ruined. It was the whales that used to drive the caplin to the land, and if one permitted the whales to be killed the cod fishery would be ruined. In a very short time no less than fourteen whalers were on this coast and Labrador. The Norwegians went into the whale fishery on an extensive scale until whale oil and seal oil sank so low in price that it would not pay to pursue the business. Many of the men who put their money in the whale fishery lost it, but the quantity of caplin held good and our floaters in Labrador are getting more and more fish every year.

The price of our cod oil sank so low that many of our best fishermen last year threw away their liver, contending that the oil would not pay for the cost of the casks. The cost of oil has gone up this year 100 per cent. Seal oil became so cheap that when the sealers in 1902 heard that the price of seals would be only $3 they went on strike and held up the entire fleet for forty-eight hours until they were promised $3.50 per cwt. The price the sealers agreed on this spring was $3 per cwt., exactly the same price they struck on in 1902, but fortunately on our return this year the price was $3.50, exactly the same as it was in 1902. There was no talk of a strike this year because there was no chance of doing anything; if there was anything better for our men to do they would not continue longer at the cod or seal fishery at these low prices.

Unfortunately our Government cannot seem to see any way of getting our people productive labour, and every device to engage more men in the fishery means more fish and a smaller price. I must point out here that that letter which Mr. Devine had published the other day coming from Mr. Howley was one of many published on the same subject forty years ago. The building of the railway, the cutting of sleepers and other work was the only thing that saved the situation—thousands of men withdrew from the fisheries which made it better for those who remained at that work, and temporary prosperity was the result.

The advocates of the railway shouted that the revenue was going up by leaps and bounds, as was really the case; but most of those who did the shouting were either blind to the true state of affairs or for other reasons kept back the truth and did not tell the people that our apparent prosperity was only fictitious and obtained with borrowed money, and the so-called prosperity we were enjoying then would act like a millstone around the necks of generations to come. The bubble burst two years ago when our public debt became so great that we could borrow no more, and we are now bitterly reminded of that old adage, "Marry in haste, repent at leisure."

Such letters as Mr. Howley and others wrote advising a portion of our men to get back to the land were lost sight of in the mad desire to borrow money, swell our revenue and get rich quick. Consequently Mr. Howley's letter the other day was like a bolt from the blue or a nail driven in a sure place, and I believe whole-heartedly that in getting a portion of our people back to the land lies our only hope in getting back to prosperity. I admit it will take a long time, but the quicker it is begun the quicker will the goal be reached.

Mr. Ford recently said that "The worker wants a chance to get back to the land. That is where real security and real happiness will be found. The working man and the countryman should have one foot on the land and one foot in industry." Mr. Ford has enlarged upon these views from time to time. He has said: "Mass production was not a mistake but it might be a mistake to prolong it. We can now take what we have learned in crowded industrial centres and use it to good advantage in bettering conditions in the village. Breaking up huge plants into many small ones will free society from doles and unemployment and give greater stability to the buying power of workers. We have been over-emphasizing the importance of money. We have not given proper attention to sane, clean living. Nothing contributes to an appreciation of real values so much as profitable living in the open country or in small communities. Although we have been thinking otherwise, we must recognize that after all land is the essential basis of our national security."

The above statement reminds me of the demand our longshoremen are making today about their right to handle freight here in St. John's on board our coasting schooners. Without entering into the merits of the case at all—as I think both parties are well able to put their cases for themselves—I submit that the real cause of the trouble is that there are two or three times as many longshoremen in St. John's as are needed for the amount of work available. Their real friend is the person who can remove them from this city to some other locality where they can earn a living for themselves and their families. To permit their surplus number to go on board these coasting schooners, where freight rates are already so low that they at their best can only get a new shilling for an old one, would only make matters worse.

The only two fisheries in Newfoundland that I have not discussed are mackerel and lobster. I will deal with mackerel firstly. About a hundred and twenty years ago mackerel were so plentiful in Newfoundland that they were a menace to the cod fishery. The only way to dispose of them was to salt them. They had become so plentiful that their value was almost nil. When the fishermen threw out their bait for codfish it would be devoured by mackerel; suddenly they almost disappeared. Science was not so far advanced in those days as it is now, and people were a little more superstitious, so that it was said that the mackerel were damned off the coast. During the last two or three years mackerel have been found on our coast, but salted mackerel is the same as salted salmon—it is not worth the catching. Nova Scotia and the United States still do a big mackerel business, but they dispose of these, fresh.

Seventy years ago the canning of lobster was unknown in Newfoundland. The first indication we would get of lobsters would be in April in seal nets. After eating all we wanted for food, the rest would be given to pigs. Later in the summer they became a great menace to fishermen by getting into their cod nets. I knew one man to take 500 out of one fleet of nets. About sixty or sixty-five years ago, people commenced canning lobsters in Bonavista Bay. If I mistake not, a man called Treadwell, belonging to Nova Scotia, started a canning factory at Pool's Island and, not knowing the quantity of lobsters around that place, he employed a lot of servants to hook lobsters at so much in wages and so much per hundred lobsters. The lobsters kept coming in, and it was soon found that the number of hands engaged at the factory could not handle anything like the quantity that was hooked. As a result, the servants insisted on his taking their lobsters, as they were paid by the hundred until a certain time. A very large quantity was packed and tens of thousands of lobsters were thrown away, for pigs to eat and for manure for gardens.

Subsequently local factories were started, and ten years later eleven factories were packing lobsters on the same ground. They did not, however, get near the quantity packed by Treadwell in his first summer, to say nothing of what was thrown away. Such was the history of the lobster fishery in Newfoundland, and no attempt was made by the Governments of Newfoundland to lock the stable door until the horse had made its escape and then the door was barred and bolted. A close season for three years was made and other precautions were taken after the close season, but the lobster fishery of Newfoundland is today but the miniature of what it was fifty years ago.

A word about the squid will not perhaps be out of place here. In the past we used them only as bait to catch codfish, but recently they have become valuable as a food product for the Chinese. The people on the south side of Bonavista Bay particularly have done a good business for the last few years, and even now they are offering $6 per barrel for them. The squid is of a suicidal turn of mind, and in some years they come to our shores in millions so that we can get not only all we want for bait but all we want to dry. Millions run on the shores, and when the tide runs out they are found dead. They are also extremely haphazard in their habits. Neither winds nor currents affect them, and even the scientist at Bay Bulls cannot keep track of them or advise the fishermen where to go to locate them.

These few remarks conclude what I propose to say about the fisheries of Newfoundland. What I have said is backed up by over sixty years of experience, over a half century of which was devoted to a very serious consideration of the problems of this country. For the first twenty years of my life I was like most young men of today, drifting along comfortably on the doctrine, "The Lord will provide." A far more profitable philosophy was expounded by the Rev. Charles Lynch a few years ago when he was a passenger with me on board the *S.S. Prospero*. We had some college students on board, and one morning when I went on the bridge I overheard the conversation. Mr. Lynch was giving the students some advice; It was this:

"If you want to see a town,
The sort of a town you like,
You needn't pack your clothes
In a grip,
And go off on a long, long hike.
You'll only find what you left behind,
There is nothing really new.
It's a knock at yourself, then a knock at your town;
It isn't your town, it's you.

Towns are not made
Of men who are afraid
That somebody else will get ahead.

It's when you do your personal stake,
And your neighbours do one too,
That you see the town you want to see;
It isn't your town, it's you."

THE *S.S. NEWFOUNDLAND* IN THE ICE, SKIPPERED BY CAPTAIN WESTBURY KEAN IN THE GREAT 1914 SEALING DISASTER. (PHOTO: CENTRE FOR NEWFOUNDLAND STUDIES ARCIVES)

CHAPTER XIII

A dry dock—The railway—Newfoundland's plight

I now propose to deal with the hope our legislators had of building a railway and a dry dock in St. John's. I cannot do better than quote the words of Sir F. B. Carter on the proposed building of the dry dock:

"The dock is to be of such dimensions that it can accommodate the largest oceanic steamers, being 600 feet in length, 100 feet in breadth and 26 feet in depth. The Government have agreed to give a subsidy of $30,000 per annum for forty-five years, thus securing interest at 5 per cent. on $600,000. The total cost is estimated at $1,000,000. This dock will be of vast importance to disabled steamers and vessels requiring repairs, great numbers of which seek this port from all parts of the Atlantic. It will also serve for the repairing of the fleet of twenty-five steamers and the large numbers of sailing vessels, which are connected with St. John's itself. It seems clear from all these facts that Newfoundland has at length fairly moved into the paths of progress and has a bright and prosperous future opening before her. Her great natural resources will now be turned to account and her inhabitants will advance in the arts and appliances of civilized life. The population according to the last census was 161,000; it is now probably 185,000. This small population is sprinkled round the shores of an island one-sixth larger than Ireland and having an area of 42,000 square miles. That it will become an attractive field for emigration cannot be doubted, when once the interior valleys are rendered fairly accessible by road and rail."

It is very evident from this quotation that Sir F. B. Carter concluded that the building of the railway and the building of a dry dock in St. John's was the parting of the ways for Newfoundland. He knew the obstacles that were thrown in the way of agriculture in this country, and he was thoroughly acquainted with similar letters to that written by Mr. Howley and published the other day in our daily papers. He had also read the following Hatton & harvey's "History of Newfoundland":

"So strong was the feeling against Newfoundland at the date referred to (that was in 1813) that permission to cultivate the soil, for which the people had long been begging, was at first granted reluctantly and accomplished with such restrictions that it was impossible for agriculture to make any great advances. There were no roads, nor any prospect of any being constructed; and only small plots of ground four acres in extent were granted on lease of twenty or thirty years, and subject to a quit-rent of two shillings and sixpence per acre to ten and even twenty shillings per annum.

"Despite these unfavourable conditions, the number of applications for land was greater than could be met. In contrast to this hard usage was the policy pursued by the British Government at the same time, in promoting the settlement of the neighbouring provinces of Nova Scotia, New Brunswick and other parts of Canada. Millions of money were lavished by Government in promoting the settlement of these colonies. Large grants of land were offered free of charge; settlers were advertised for; their expenses were paid, means were provide for their subsistence, until the land made returns; hundreds of miles of roads were constructed; canals were made and harbours were improved and fortified; on the other hand, not only was there no help given to Newfoundland, but a heavy rent was charged for small patches of land, let on short leases. Every improvement was accomplished by the hard toil of the settlers themselves, not only without assistance but in opposition to the wretched policy of the Government."

Now let us see what Mr. Murray, the geological surveyor, says as late as 1878:

"The magnificent pine forests are left to rot or perish by fire, the soil is fertile enough to sustain many thousands of our people in comfort but it is as yet untouched by plough or spade. The forest primeval shows no clearing won by human industry. All is primitive wilderness."

It may seem surprising that such should be the plight of an island only five days' steaming distance from Great Britain, and with thousands of emigrants passing these shores every day to seek a home in the far west of America, but it must be remembered that until recently the very existence of Newfoundland's fertile lands and valuable forests was unknown. Now that great revolutionary, the Railway, is about to penetrate the wastes, a portion of the great stream of emigration will ere long be diverted towards these untenanted regions, which by human industry may be made to blossom like the rose. To quote from a speech which I delivered on the third paragraph in the speech from the Throne relating to the Empire Marketing Board in February, 1932:

"Personally, if I went to the Empire Marketing Board I would put up a colonization scheme before them. I would try to enter into an agreement by which they would send some of their unemployed people possessed with a knowledge of farming, and I would offer them free tracts of fertile land to settle on, and I would try to induce about 10,000 of our fishermen to settle among them and learn the art of cultivation of the soil and growing for ourselves the products of the farm, which we now import from Prince Edward's Island and other parts of Nova Scotia. I would give every encouragement to raise our own cattle to take the place of what we now import from New Zealand, Canada and other countries."

Every time our fisheries have failed either in quantity or price for the last hundred years our people have been forced to starvation conditions. For the last fifty years we have relieved the tension by borrowing money for public works, and while we have been warned again and again by some of our best public men, one Government has tried to outdo the other as to who would borrow the most, until 1931, when our credit was stopped in the foreign markets of the world. A policy of retrenchment has been forced upon us, and I maintain that we ought not to go into any other speculation until order is restored out of chaos.

The last authority is Mr. Fraser Rae, who visited this island in 1880 and who has recorded his views in an excellent and trustworthy book, "Newfoundland to Manitoba."

"The customs returns for 1880 show that in that year the total value of agricultural produce imported into Newfoundland was no less than $2,825,411. If we suppose this amount of produce raised in the country, which, were the island opened up to any extent, would be the case, then nearly three millions of dollars annually, which are now sent out of the country to pay the agriculturalist of other places, would be retained and spent among Newfoundland farmers, to the great benefit of the home population. If the encouragement of home manufactures is proper, then as farms are food factories, every facility should be given for the extension of this industry, by providing railways for the transport of farm produce to market. It is evident from these returns that for the produce of the farm and dairy and the raising of stock, there will be, for years to come, a remunerative market in the island itself, apart altogether from exportation."

It is abundantly clear, therefore, from the arguments advanced for the building of a railway in this country, that the main attraction was the development of agricultural pursuits. The staunchest advocates of the railway had visions that thousands of emigrants would flock here and make their homes in this country and help to bear their share of taxation and lessen the load we had to bear. The railway came, but it did not bring with it the desired results. The only gain that came to us was that it gave labour while it was under construction. As soon as the work was finished, however, hundreds of people were thrown out of employment, and it was then the duty of the politician to stampede the Government into giving the people bread. When there is enough poverty two or three politicians with glib tongues can always get the people with them and stampede a Government into action.

WITH THE CRY "OLD AND YOUNG AHEAD" THE SEALERS WENT OVER THE SIDE ONTO THE ICE TO HARVEST SEALS. (PHOTO: CENTRE FOR NEWFOUNDLAND STUDIES ARCHIVES)

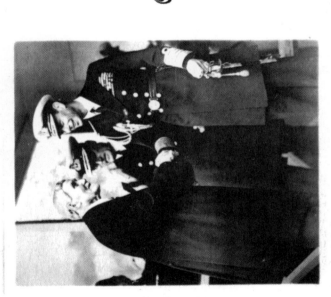

Season's
Greetings
from

Capt. The Hon. Abraham Kean, O.B.E.

Being presented to
His Majesty King George VI,
in the presence of
His Excellency Governor Walwyn,
on the occasion of Their Majesties'
visit to Newfoundland, June 17th 1939.

CAPTAIN ABRAM KEAN'S CHRISTMAS CARD. COURTESY MADELINE (KEAN) GOSSE.

CHAPTER XIV

The two banks—An historical snapshot—A load of debt—The Commission of Government's task—The bank crash

I now propose to take you back to 1880, or fifty-four years ago. I want to point out at the outset that there was then no public debt. We had two banks, one called the Union Bank and the other the Commercial Bank.

The following is the report on the Union Bank on the 1st of December, 1880:

"The Union Bank of Newfoundland is one of the most prosperous banking institutions now in existence. It was established in 1854. During the first eighteen years it paid an average dividend and bonus of 11 1/2 per cent per annum. The reserve fund was then so large that the Directors declared a special bonus of 50 per cent, which was taken by the shareholders in paid-up shares. On this increased capital the dividends and bonuses have of late years been 20 per cent per annum or to original shareholders equivalent to 27 per cent on their investment. The original $200 share now sells for $800."

"The Commercial Bank is also a very prosperous institution. It was established in 1857. Its original $200 share now sells for $520. In dividends and bonuses its rate of interest now averages 12 per cent per annum. Its capital is Pounds (L)50,000. Both banks have been conducted with great skill and prudence. Neither engages in any speculative business, all transactions being of the safe and solid order."

Such was the position of our two banks as stated in Hatton & Harvey's "History of Newfoundland."

The railway went through the district of Harbour Main. The people abandoned their fisheries and received payment in cash for their labour. For four years Harbour Main was the most flourishing district in the country. The first railway contract, known as the Blackman Contract, failed, however, before they reached Harbour Grace, and when the General Election took place in 1885 a party known as the Reform party, led by Robert Thorburn (afterwards Sir Robert Thorburn), defeated the great Liberal party by a sweeping majority. At their first party meeting the urgent need of doing something for the people of the Harbour Main district was discussed and took us all by surprise. After some discussion it was agreed that whatever sum was voted for Harbour Main per head, a similar sum would be voted for all the other districts. Borrowing had commenced under the great Liberal party!

It was followed by the Tory party. The second year of the Thorburn party, Robert Bond, with A. B. Morine and Thomas Murphy were in opposition. Robert Bond introduced the Ballot Act, which was defeated that year, was taken up by the Government party in the following year and passed by a unanimous vote. In 1889 at the next General Election the Thorburn Government returned only one man. Sir William Whiteway and the great Liberal party came back to power, apparently stronger than ever, and those who had for a long time advocated the Ballot Act were jubilant. Their jubilation was, however, short-lived, for the Opposition filed petitions against them and most of them were unseated for bribery and corruption. Such was their power over the people, however, that they got substitutes to take their places and held Government until 1894, when on November the 9th [sic], henceforth known as Black Monday, both banks closed their doors and went into insolvency. Many of our large business concerns had so much money on paper that most of them were crippled to such an extent that temporary suspension was the outcome. The firm of Bowring Brothers issued their own cheques, which were looked upon as being as good as gold, and it will be long before their action will be forgotten. Consternation reigned for a time, but Robert Bond, who was then Colonial Secretary, went to England and secured a loan of $2,000,000. On his return, he was welcomed by a torchlight procession. If the torchlight bearers could have known then as we know now what use was made of the millions that have been borrowed from time to time, every man would have had crêpe (a black arm band) on his arm instead of a torch in his hand.

In 1897 Sir James Winter led another party and came back victorious, but although the Liberal party was defeated, Sir Robert Bond was elected, together with several others of the party. In 1898 millions more were borrowed, but not one dollar was spent in carrying out the original object of the railway, namely, the fostering of agricultural pursuits, or the provision of the means for growing farm produce or raising cattle to take the place of what we were importing from foreign countries. Reid's were given a very large contract in connection with the Coastal Service and a further extension of the railway, and although it was on the same principle of the '98 Contract given by the Liberal party themselves, the Opposition, led by Sir Robert Bond, started a cry that the Government party, led by Sir James Winter, was giving all the land in the country to the Reid's.

In 1889 [sic; 1900] Sir Robert Bond moved a vote of no confidence in the Government. Some of the Government party crossed the floor and voted with the Opposition and defeated the Government. One of them said that to sit with such a Government was to him like hell on earth. Little did he know when he uttered these words that history would repeat itself, for the fate of the Winter party also overtook that led by Sir Robert Bond. In 1908 railways were built to give labour to the people to supply their present wants. When the work was finished the people returned to their former homes less able to catch fish than those who had continued in that business and more dissatisfied with themselves. When the people are dissatisfied the politician gets dissatisfied also. The great Liberal party became divided—one of their Executive, Mr. Morris (now Lord Morris) led a party which he called the People's party and sought the support of the people against the party led by Sir Robert Bond. The result was that out of a House of thirty-six representatives, both parties came back with eighteen. They agreed to vote a certain sum of money to carry on the affairs of the country, and renewed the contest for a General Election in the spring.

Morris outlined his policy, however, as one of progress, assuring the people that if he were returned he would give employment to the people by building branch railways. He came back victorious and carried out his promise and built branch railways. It had the same effect as all other works of that kind as long as the money holds out. People had plenty, the spending of the money automatically swelled the revenue, and the same old cry was raised, "We must be better off because the revenue is greater."

From the time the first sum of money was borrowed until 1909 we had seven Prime Ministers and borrowed millions of dollars. Not one settlement was, however, established, unless you call Whitbourne an agricultural settlement. What took place subsequently? If the Governments of the first eighteen years whipped us with serpents, those that followed whipped us with scorpions until between them they had piled up a huge public debt amounting to $100,000,000, and left us in a bankrupt condition.

The Commission of Government sees no other course open this year but to do what former Governments have done in this country for the last three hundred years, namely, to get all the people fishing. Although we are prepared to admit that little else could be done this year, we sincerely hope that this is but a stop-gap and not a permanent policy. It is nonsense for us to talk about not borrowing more money. In our present condition, if we do not borrow we neither dare to hold on nor to let go.

After writing the above I received a copy of the *Daily News* from which I clipped the following:

"The Commission of Government has a definite agricultural policy, and the Commissioner will confer with the Department of Agriculture, with a view to securing assistance in carrying out this policy."

We hope they will study local conditions carefully and wish them success in their new venture. Naturally, I am not in a position to write further on this subject, as I have not the remotest idea of what their agricultural policy will be. Before closing this chapter, however, it only fair to say that the Government led by Lord Morris in 1909 instituted for the first time a Newfoundland Board of Trade. As there was no source of revenue except the regular fee, after the first years membership began to dwindle and financial difficulties were very much in evidence.

A few years ago, however, new life was infused into it, and some of our young men took a hand. It is now presided over by one of our young lawyers, Mr. R. Gushue, who had the honour last year of being the first President to hold office for two consecutive years. With a young live-wire, Mr. H. Mews, as Secretary, and a splendid staff of Councillors, many of our leading merchants and former Presidents, a *Journal of Commerce* is printed every month. The debt of the Board has been wiped out; an account of the proceedings is published every month, in striking contrast to twenty years ago when all transactions were behind closed doors and the actions of those in charge gave it the appearance of a secret society rather than an institution to foster trade and give public information. While I was Councillor and President I attempted to establish a spirit of mutual confidence. Let us hope that the good work now going on in the Board of Trade will continue and that hundreds of others will join and make their power for good felt in the land.

In discussing the bank crash I spoke of it only in relation to the Governments and the building of railways. There is a much more important aspect, and one which will merit public attention.

From my standpoint the bank crash was a blessing in disguise to the fishermen of this country. It marked the breakdown of a long-standing custom of the credit system, which may have had some good points but had its day, and was no longer in keeping with the conditions of the latter part of the nineteenth century. The custom of giving a merchant all your earnings and then taking all your needs from him often brought trouble on both sides. If a customer did well and had a good voyage of fish, there was the temptation on the part of the merchant to entice the dealer to purchase as much as possible, as it would be like gall and wormwood to pay out cash to one of their dealers when there were so many more of them who would not be able to square their accounts.

Those, on the other hand, who had already more than they could pay, wanted to get more than they would be able to pay and far more than the merchant intended they should get, and had got already more than the merchants expected they would pay for. Consequently, when the bank crash came, the merchants owed the banks so much that they could not pay their debts and had to go into insolvency. On the other hand, it was disclosed that what the merchants owed the banks was owed by the fishermen to the merchants. The crux of the whole matter was that the fisherman could no more pay for larger vessels than their fathers could on the fisheries alone, and a great many of the fishermen owed the merchants more on the schooners and outfits, of which they were the nominal owners, than they could ever hope to pay off in a lifetime. On the one hand, there was a feeling that the fishermen did not care if they every paid their debts or not; on the other hand, there was a feeling that the merchants had lots of money and were a hard-hearted lot, who gloried in making the fishermen of Newfoundland their slaves for ever. Sad to relate, many who should have known better encouraged that feeling.

The bank crash came as a surprise to both sides. What was to be done? Many of our large supplying firms were the owners of the fishermen's schooners. No other merchant could get these schooners until a settlement was made with their former owners. The merchants were willing to hand over to the banks the property they had on hand, in vessels, traps and gear. No one would think of paying one-tenth of what the fishermen owed on the schooners, but on the other hand, the banks had to take what they could get. The fishermen took care that they secured a complete release from their former merchant for whatever the new merchants would pay for their outfit. The result was that some of the greatest bargains were had.

Many of the fishermen, who were the nominal owners of these vessels, got clear of thousands of dollars of debt for a few hundred; after one or two years these men were the owners of all their property and independent men, which they never could have been if there had been no bank crash. Three Canadian banks on Water Street took the place of the two defunct banks on the hill. The method of banking was on a much improved plan, which the people were not slow to learn.

The twenty years, from 1890 to 1910, were the most successful in the history of steamers at the seal fishery. A much improved class of schooners was bought and built for carrying on the cod fishery. The fishermen built better houses than they had heretofore, and much better than their fathers had; they also had much better furniture—piano and organ took the places of concertina and jew's harp. After the bank crash a small portion of the fishermen joined Sir William Coaker and built premises at Port Union, besides branch stores in most of the outports, at a cost of some hundreds of thousands of dollars—more dollars than they could have found cents before the bank crash. Borrowing money for the building of railways provided winter employment; people became more prosperous, built better houses and wore better clothes. They bought the best food, and general prosperity became the order of the day.

On the 4th of August, 1914, Germany declared war against England and her Allies. Recruits were wanted; our men were not slow in rallying to the defence of the flag that had flown so long to the battle and the breeze. Those who were accepted and put under arms were also put under wages. The young and middle-aged went to the war, the old remained to keep the home fires burning. We still kept the fishery in working order, the price of fish and oil exceeding in price anything previously heard of in the history of the industry. Four years of unprecedented prosperity followed and, instead of saving for the aftermath of the war, extravagance and sport became commonplace. But the end of prosperity came, and with it came the years of depression. The greater part of the nations of the world took part in the Great War—all who did are looking for a way out the depression, and it would be presumption on my part even to suggest a remedy. I think we may all draw inspiration from the poet as to the course we should follow individually:

> "New occasions teach new duties.
> Time makes ancient truth uncouth,
> But we must ever up and onward
> Who would keep abreast of truth.
>
> Though the cause of evil triumph,
> Yet 'tis truth alone is strong,
> Though its portion be the scaffold,
> And upon the throne be wrong.
>
> Yet the truth shall sway the future,
> And behind the dim unknown
> Standeth God within the shadow,
> Keeping watch above His own."

With these words I shall close this chapter. The last portion of this work deals with the accomplishment of a world's record in bringing to port 1,008,000 seals in practically forty-five years, as I want all those of my crew who helped me to accomplish that feat to share with me in the congratulations.

Some parts of this book are mere tabulations of events, but from them we can perhaps learn valuable object lessons. Governments were brought into power by majority votes and defeated by a similar vote, which does not mean majorities are right. On the contrary, almost all the good that has come to us has come to us by minorities. W. E. Gladstone has said: "I painfully reflect that in almost every political controversy of the last fifty years the leisured classes, the titled classes, the wealthy classes, the educated classes have been in the wrong. The common people, the toilers, the men of common sense—these have been responsible for nearly all the social reform measures which the world accepts today."

The value Judas placed upon his Master when he sold Him for thirty pieces of silver was out of all proportion to His true worth, and he set far too high a value on the benefits to himself of the thirty pieces of silver. It did not take long for him to find out his mistake, but instead of seeking forgiveness he made the second blunder by going out and hanging himself. Is it not a fact today that many of our people set far too low an estimate on character? They go around begging their friends to give them recommendations to get positions, and are often discharged for smuggling cigarettes or liquour into the country to defraud the customs. Pilate set far too low a value on character when he delivered up an innocent person to the Jews to be crucified, not without some pain of conscience, 'tis true, for he called for water to wash his hands to free himself from the guilt. It did not work, however, for he had branded himself as a coward and unfit to hold such a responsible position.

$\mathcal{F}$LIPPER $\mathcal{S}$UPPER

GIVEN BY
METHODIST COLLEGE LITERARY INSTITUTE
AT PITTS MEMORIAL HALL
TUESDAY, MAY 1st 1934
IN HONOUR OF HON. CAPTAIN A. KEAN

An active member of the Institute, to mark his outstanding
achievement in bringing to port in ships under his
command over one million seals.

TOAST LIST

"THE KING"

Prop.	Resp
The Chairman	The National Anthem

"HON CAPT. KEAN"

The Chairman - - - - - Hon. Capt. Kean

The following speakers will be associated
with this Toast:

Hon. Mr. Justice Higgins
C. E. Hunt, Esq., K. C.
H. G. R. Mews, Esq.

❖

GROUP SIGNING
Musical items under direction of
Mr. H. Gordon Christian, L.R.A M.

GOD SAVE THE KING

A. Kean

1007319   1007319

"NEWFOUNDLAND'S MOST FAMOUS MILLIONAIRE"

FLIPPER DINNER INVITATION.
COURTESY OF MADELINE (KEAN) GOSSE.

CHAPTER XV

The millionth seal—Prayers and victory—A shower of congratulation—Gifts, bunting and a flipper dinner—O.B.E.— Conclusion

I shall devote the last chapter of this book to all those who showered their congratulations on me after it was announced that I had reached my millionth seal. But perhaps I had better explain. I met with a great set-back in 1930, when I wanted 72,428 to complete the million. For four years I was master of the *S.S. Nascopie,* one of the most powerful ice-breakers in the fleet, and averaged almost 30,000 per spring. On July of that year I made an application for the *Nascopie* for 1931. My application was accepted, but on condition that the ship would go. I had engaged my crew as in other years, and at the New Year when I made inquiry at Job Brothers, they told me they thought there was some doubt as to whether the *Nascopie* would go to the seal fishery, and thought I had better wire for information. I did so, and was told by the Hudson Bay Company that the *Nascopie* would not go that year.

My first duty was to release the crew I had engaged and let them get berths elsewhere. The only other chance was a wooden ship, the *S.S. Thetis,* in which hardly anybody would go. My best friends tried to dissuade me from going in her, saying that it would only ruin the record I had previously built up. The million seals, however, was my goal. I put in my application with several others and got her. Had I not, I should not be writing these lines now, for if I had not gone in the *Thetis* the million seals would not have been reached yet. More remarkable still, I got over 11,000 seals and my crew made the largest bill for that year.

The next year I went back again in my old ship, the *Terra Nova,* out of Bowring Brothers, but the average by the *Terra Nova* was small compared with the average of the steel ships. 1934 was ushered in and I had got my appointment for the *S.S. Terra Nova.*[1] I was still short of my million by 40,300. Nothing short of a miracle could take place whereby I could hope to reach my million in 1934. Rumour was afloat that the *S.S. Beothic* might go, and that perhaps Bowrings would charter her. I listened to every bit of gossip on the street, but could hear nothing that could brighten my hope that anything better than the *Terra Nova* awaited me. On the 1st day of February, Mr. Eric Bowring called me by telephone and asked me which ship I would like to command that year, the *Beothic* or *Terra Nova.* I replied *Beothic.*

The size of the *Beothic* was such that every doubt was removed as to reaching the million. Those interested in my reaching the million mark could not talk of anything else. All the Directors of the firm and many of the office hands all talked in terms of "The million." The President of the Board of Trade (who was also President of the M.C.L.I.) said, "If you reach your million, we will put on the biggest flipper supper ever given." Of course it was understood I was to provide the flippers. Miss Elsie Holloway, one of our best photographers, said to me, "I am sending my man over to take your picture on the bridge of the *Beothic* with your fur coat and cap on, and if you don't reach your million seals I shall be mad with you." Evidently she had caught the million craze also. On my way across to the *Beothic* I met the Rev. Canon Peile, kodak in hand, who said, "I want to take your picture on the bridge of the *Beothic* with your rig on that you wear sealing." Evidently I had received his benediction also.

Just before I sailed I received a message from a very enthusiastic friend of mine at Change Islands saying, "All Change Islands are praying for you." I replied, "Tell them to pray without ceasing." So, with all these good wishes, the prayers of all Change Islands and the help of a crew of 225 with all the skill and judgment that I could put into it, on the 2nd day of April the goal was reached, not without a great many hardships and disappointments. Hundreds who helped me to reach that goal did not share in the final victory. Only the 225 of the *Beothic's* crew did the cheering, but it could not be confined to them.

About 3 p.m. that day my operator said to me, "Captain, I heard over Ayre & Sons' radio this morning that Captain W. B. Kean (a son of mine) is going to broadcast a message to the sealers this evening at 7 p.m." I gave him a message to Bowrings: "Inform W. B. Kean that we have reached our million mark today," and at 7 p.m. I went into the operating-room and heard every word as plain as if I were in the Newfoundland Hotel.

I received my first message from Mr. John Parker, of Parker & Monroe, and the next two days messages from Captain W. C. Winsor, Admiral David Murray Anderson, Sir John Hope Simpson, Messrs. Bowring Brothers, Mr. Charles Bowring and his son in New York, the different captains in the sealing fleet, the Hon. McNamara, the President of the Board of Trade, Captain Randell and many others.

The following is a letter sent to me from the Admiral Governor of Newfoundland:

21st April, 1934.

"DEAR CAPTAIN KEAN,

You have had my congratulations on making up your total of one million seals by radio, but I feel I must again offer you my hearty congratulations on your wonderful feat. Not only is it a wonderful personal success, but by your skill and energy during your many years in command, you have brought thousands of dollars into the country and have enabled many thousands of our men to return to their homes with cheerful hearts and money to support their families.

I am sure my good wishes and earnest hope that you may be

spared for many years to go to the Ice will be echoed by all in
Newfoundland.
Believe me, with all good wishes.
Yours sincerely,
(*Signed*) D. MURRAY ANDERSON,
Admiral Governor."

We still pursued the voyage and totalled altogether 48,701,
making in all a total of 1,008,100 seals since I became a master.
We reached St. John's on April 19th and were received with
ringing cheers, the blowing of whistles and the flying of flags.
Shortly after my return from the seal fishery, Bowring Brothers
presented me with a silver seal on a pedestal, and also a very
substantial cheque. The Board of Trade presented me with a
model of the *S.S. Terra Nova* in a glass case with a silk flag,
which must have cost hundreds of dollars. Mr. Gushue, President
of the M.C.L.I., good as his word, presented me with a handsome
writing tablet. Mr. Justice Higgins, one of our most popular
Judges of the Supreme Court, Mr. Charles Hunt, a leading
lawyer, and the popular Secretary of the Board of Trade, Mr.
Harry Mews, proposed toasts to me. I think it was one of the most
pleasant evenings ever held in that building. On the 3rd of June,
when the Birthday Honours of the King were announced, I was
one of two Newfoundlanders who were remembered on that
occasion.

I trust that those who read these lines will believe me when I
say that although I worked for the million seals—it was my goal
for the last ten years—never in my wildest dreams did I expect a
Royal Honour. It has come, and I appreciate the spirit that
prompted or suggested it to His Majesty the King.

Many who have offered me their hearty congratulations were
at one time political opponents. Sir Alfred Morine and I
commenced our first political battle on opposite sides as far back
as 1885. When I came in from the ice his letter of congratulation
was awaiting me, and when I was given my O.B.E. he surpassed

himself, first in a message, then in a letter. There was also one from his son, expressing similar sentiments, which I very much appreciated.

Shortly after coming from the seal fishery I went to New York and found the same spirit prevailing; radios were catching it up from the newspapers and broadcasting it.

The following is a clipping from one of the daily papers:

CAPTAIN A. KEAN PRESENTED WITH O.B.E.

"At Government House at noon today Captain Abram Kean was presented with the Order of the British Empire by His Excellency the Governor, Admiral Sir David Anderson. The announcement of the award to Captain Kean was made some time ago and was in recognition of his success at the seal fishery, when he returned from the icefields with his millionth seal. Amongst those at the presentation were the Honourables the Commissioner for Justice and the Commissioner for Natural Resources, Mr. E. A. Bowring, Mr. James Howley, O.B.E., and members of Captain Kean's family, including his son, Captain Wes. Kean, his daughter Allie Kean, his grandson, Abraham Kean, Jr., and granddaughter, Miss Margaret Kean, Mrs. Sheppard, and Miss Madeline Kean; also Mrs. F. H. Kean, widow of the late Captain J. W. Kean."

This concludes the story of the 1,008,100 seals landed from the ships that I have commanded in forty-seven years, two years of which I was in sailing vessels, during which time I brought in 700.

I do not claim perfection for my narrative. Such as it is, with all its blemishes, it represents a sincere and careful account of fifty years in the service of my country.

The story of the million seals will soon be past history. The future is still hidden. The Bowrings, with their usual desire to keep their ships in order, have given the *S.S. Beothic* a thorough overhauling and a reclassed certificate from Lloyd's. She is more fitted for the work of sealing than ever before. If my health holds good I hope to command her for some years yet, and add considerably to my sealing record before I depart for the land where there is no more sea.

1 There is some confusion over chronology here.

THE SEALING STEAMER S.S. FLORIZEL STUCK IN THE ICE. (PHOTO: CENTRE FOR NEWFOUNDLAND STUDIES ARCHIVES)

INDEX

Jeff
Rubin

MUSICA

RZUDAS — MUN.
EVANS " STRAINED
mercy"